SECOND-CHANCE HORSES

INSPIRING STORIES OF EX-RACEHORSES SUCCEEDING IN NEW CAREERS

BY THE STAFF AND CORRESPONDENTS
OF BLOOD-HORSE PUBLICATIONS

FOREWORD BY NICK NICHOLSON

LEXINGTON, KENTUCKY

Library of Congress Control Number: 2008911904

ISBN: 978-1-58150-211-4

Printed in the United States
First Edition: 2009

a division of
Blood-Horse Publications
PUBLISHERS SINCE AI916

Contents

FOREWORD

Those fortunate enough to have owned a horse know that it can be one of the most enjoyable and satisfying aspects of their life. I have known very successful people who own large businesses, several estates, and every possible "toy," but who receive as much pleasure from owning a horse as from any other material wealth. There is something truly magical in the bond that forms between people and horses. I have seen this mystical relationship transcend people of all ages, from young girls to hardened businessmen. It cuts across different breeds of horses and a wide array of disciplines.

At its best, this relationship between a horse and its owner will truly enhance a person's life and provide for healthy and happy horses. At the very core of all of this joy and pleasure, however, is a deep responsibility. Along with the thrill of owning a horse comes the commitment to its care, health, and well-being. Simply put, you can't have one without the other. The stories in *Second-Chance Horses* make that clear. Not only have the ex-racehorses profiled in these chapters escaped uncertain fates to succeed in second careers but their owners and caretakers have become better people in giving these horses new beginnings.

This special relationship between a person and a horse, of caring for and enriching each other's lives, is one close to Keeneland's heart. Keeneland supports the broad-based effort of ensuring that racehorses have dignified lives once their careers on the track are over.

We hope you enjoy these inspiring stories. Proceeds received by Keeneland from the sale of this book will be donated to organizations and individuals that are finding appropriate homes for horses in need of loving care.

Nick Nicholson
President and CEO
Keeneland Association

BANION

BY RENA BAER

1

There's no question that Banion is beloved at Central Kentucky Riding for Hope, where he is a mainstay in its equine therapy programs, but there is a question about who the Thoroughbred really is.

Common sense tells me he's a twenty-four-year-old former racehorse named Banyan House who plied his trade on Kentucky tracks for a few years. But the ID number tattooed inside his lip matches that of Hurry to Flag, a nineteen-year-old Thoroughbred who once raced on the dusty tracks of Texas and Oklahoma. And, surely, the tattoo must be right?

Well, a lot of years have passed, and tattoos can get more difficult to read as they fade with time. And, unfortunately, the physical descriptions on their pedigrees identify each as being dark brown. Listening to the former trainers talk about each of the horses' good natures and tall, lanky frames — it sounds like they are describing the same horse.

I started researching this story going out to the Riding for Hope program at the Kentucky Horse Park to visit the horse I had been assigned to write about. As they brought him out for a look-see, a staff member handed me a printout of his pedigree and told me he was a former racehorse named Hurry to Flag. He was very peaceful and at ease as we all fawned over him. He's a gentle 17-hand gelding blind in his left eye and with only limited vision in his right. His back is starting to sway slightly, but his nature is not old.

He is a social horse whose perceptive instincts make him an ideal equine assistant for non-mounted therapy. When someone in the program is learning how to care for horses and lacks confidence, the staff at Riding for Hope say Banion is a patient teacher, withstanding awkward movements with aplomb and affording a beginner the same respect as a seasoned veteran. If he senses someone is in a cheerful mood, he's more than ready to play, nudging them with his nose and nickering. And when he sees that someone is sad, he offers comfort by standing quietly beside the person.

Program director Denise Spittler told me that Hospice uses Riding for Hope's non-mounted therapy to help people who are grieving. A bereavement counselor will come out with someone who has lost a loved one. The two will talk as they decorate Banion's tail and mane with colorful beads. He'll stand quietly between them, enjoying the attention, and helping facilitate the counseling session with his presence alone. The conversation flows more naturally over a peaceful horse outside a barn on a sunny Kentucky day than in an office somewhere.

"Program participants and volunteers are always telling the Riding for Hope staff how special Banion is," said Spittler.

He's been in the program a couple of years and he's a shining example of a former racehorse that has gone on to a purpose-filled new life. But his story, I learned, is really a lot more compelling than that.

In researching Hurry to Flag's breeding and racing career, I found

Banion, with Denise Spittler, enjoys attention.

out that no one remembers him at the Anson, Texas, farm where he was bred and raced more than a decade ago. He was bred by Hassel R. Spraberry, a building contractor who with his wife, Bonnie, owned Hi-Lo Farm. The couple always kept a few broodmares at the fifteen-acre farm, breeding them and keeping some of the offspring to race.

"Hassel loved to watch them being born, raise them and feed them, and then put them in training and watch them run," Bonnie Spraberry told me about her husband, who died of cancer in 1995. She now runs the farm with her son, and though neither remembers Hurry to Flag, records show he was the product of their broodmare Hurry to Play being bred to Lt. Flag in 1988 for a $500 stud fee.

Hurry to Flag was born on March 16, 1989, at the Spraberry's Hi-Lo

Farm, named for the highs and lows of horse racing. The Spraberrys and their trainer at the time, Jack Fry, first raced him in late 1991 at Trinity Meadows Raceway, which had just opened that year in Weatherford, Texas. The minor-league track, which is now a training track, drew a decent-sized crowd, sometimes reaching 20,000, and owners and trainers fondly remember it as a nice meet in its day.

For the Spraberrys, though, Hurry to Flag quickly proved at Trinity Meadows to be more adept at providing the lows in their farm's name rather than the highs. He finished in the back of the field in his five maiden special weight races at distances between five and 7½ furlongs. His best performance as a two-year-old came in a maiden claiming race in which he finished fifth.

As a three-year-old, Hurry to Flag wound up in the hands of owner Scott Miller, scoring his first win while running in a six-furlong maiden claiming race on May 13, 1992. The colt raced fifteen times that year, primarily at Trinity Meadows, bringing home a second victory there under trainer Dickie Brown, in a 5½-furlong allowance race on September 12 and running to a third-place finish six days later in a 6½-furlong claiming race at Remington Park in Oklahoma.

I caught up with Brown, who remembers Hurry to Flag fondly, not so much for his skills as a racehorse — though he did say he was decent at short distances — but for his good nature and smooth ride. "I lived on a cattle ranch near Tulsa, and I would run him out in the pasture," said Brown, who still trains racehorses at Blue Ribbon Downs in Oklahoma. "He was such a nice horse that I could ride him across creeks and push the cows up with him.

"I could do just about anything with him," he said. "He was different."

Injuries prevented Hurry to Flag from racing until late July 1993. He ran his first race that year with Skip Lawrence listed as his owner. He was claimed back by Miller, who ran him twice in August before Lawrence claimed him back from Miller to get Hurry to Flag's only finish in the money that year — a third in a claiming race. Lawrence ran him three more times with Brown remaining the horse's trainer the whole time.

I asked Brown whether it was a friendly tug-of-war between Miller and Lawrence. No, he said, they both really liked and wanted that horse.

In the end, Brown told me, injuries forced Lawrence to sell Hurry to Flag, though he's not sure to whom.

Meanwhile, I had begun backtracking Banion's history from Riding for Hope, eagerly anticipating the place where the two stories would come together. First I talked to Tina Cassar, the vet for Riding for Hope, who was instrumental in bringing Banion to the program. She had learned about him from Ben Stivers, a fellow equine vet at Hagyard Equine Medical Institute in Lexington, who had ridden him as a trail horse until he got too busy with work. When Cassar heard Stivers describe Banion, she thought he sounded ideal for the Riding for Hope program.

Upon meeting Banion, Cassar said she found the horse in good condition. She described him as "inquisitive and intelligent. Not a donkey head. He's a fun, easy horse, like a big kid inside, but with a lot more maturity."

I called Stivers, who told me he had been relieved to find a good home for his horse. Banion had been a delight to trail ride despite his vision problems, but work had gotten too hectic and Stivers didn't want the social horse to live out his life in a field by himself, especially as he was an exceptional horse that looked out for his rider. He recalled how he had been riding Banion through overgrown fields and brush when Banion's foot became entangled in some old wire fencing. Rather than try to bolt or rear, like most horses would, particularly higher-strung Thoroughbreds, Banion came to a complete standstill, lifting his hoof and standing quietly until Stivers could extricate him.

"I knew then what a good horse he was," Stivers said.

He told me he had gotten Banion from clients Steve and Debbie Jackson. The couple, who also race Thoroughbreds, rode him for years as a hunter and were distraught when leptospirosis, an infectious disease that may cause some serious health problems, began robbing Banion of his vision. They called Stivers about euthanizing Banion, and the vet instead offered to give him a home. When I talked to Steve Jackson, he said the last thing he had ever wanted for Banion was a bleak existence, and when the leptospirosis that had blinded his left eye began to creep into his right eye, Jackson felt grim about what the future held.

"I didn't want such a great horse to suffer," he told me.

Jackson said Banion had been a magnificent hunter. "He was the epitome of a horse that had a much more fabulous second career than first career," Jackson said. "And now it's phenomenal he's at Riding for Hope."

I asked Jackson where he had gotten Banion, and he told me Midway College's equestrian program, where his wife worked at the time. Jackson said the horse wasn't working out for the program, so he took him home and within a couple of months had him broken as a hunter.

Later he said he found out Banion had been trained as a racehorse by the father of a friend.

"So did you know Dickie Brown, Jack Fry, or the Spraberrys who bred him out in Texas?" I asked him.

"No," Jackson told me, "He was bred and owned by Alex Campbell."

"Are you sure?" I asked. "His tattoo identifies him as Hurry to Flag."

"Yes, I'm sure," he told me. "We called him Banion because his name as a racehorse was Banyan House. You need to check with The Jockey Club."

His story made sense. No gaps. No periods during which he was unaccounted for and a plausible explanation for the name Banion. But still there was the question of the tattoo. Plus, I'd seen Banion. He certainly did not look or act like a twenty-four-year-old horse, and Pat Kline, director of Riding for Hope, said the vets had estimated his age more in line with Hurry to Flag than Banyan House.

A call to The Jockey Club, which I thought would clear things up for sure, only further muddied the waters. It turned out that Banyan House's tattoo number was very close to that of Hurry to Flag; only the first letter and an additional number separated the two. It seemed like more than coincidence that four numbers were the same; but it also seemed unlikely that if those four digits were still readable and accurate, wouldn't the first letter and the absence of a last number also still be discernable?

It was a frustrating place to be when I needed to write a definitive life story about a single racehorse that had gone on to a new career. I started thinking that perhaps I needed to have their foal registration photos dug out from the recesses of The Jockey Club files to see which horse more closely resembled Banion.

But thinking more about it, I decided I wasn't sure I wanted to know. During my research I had grown fond of the story of the gangly Texas cow horse who had somehow found his way to Kentucky and then to the Riding for Hope program. Still, I couldn't deny common sense, and the story wouldn't be complete unless I found out a little bit about Banyan House's history and how he wound up at Midway College.

Peggy Entrekin, who is now executive director of the United States Pony Club, had been an instructor at Midway's equestrian program and said she remembered Banion well. He was one of six former race-horses she had inherited with the program.

"He'd been taken in as a young horse that wasn't making it on the track," she told me. "We used him for three years, but he was not an easy jumper.

"It wasn't that he was trying to be a bad horse," she said. "He was actually sweet and easygoing. It's just that when he'd get to a jump he'd pile up."

When I asked her to explain, she said unless he was set up perfectly to go over a fence, it wasn't going to be a smooth or pretty jump, and his riders often ended up unseated.

When I told her what Banion was up to, she sounded glad.

"It shows that Thoroughbred people are involved in a lot of things and are not just throwing horses away after they are done at the race-track, like a lot of people think," she said.

She said she didn't remember exactly who gave Banion to the pro-gram, but she thinks he arrived in 1991, which would fit in with the story of Banyan House, who last raced in 1990. According to Jockey Club records, he was bred by Alex Campbell Jr., who owned him throughout his racing career. Campbell, a prominent Lexington businessman who is now in his early eighties, has been in the racing business for nearly half a century and has campaigned many stakes winners, though Banyan House was not one of them.

Banyan House, out of Key Move and by Erins Isle, was foaled March 18, 1985. The story that came with him is that he was named for a favorite vacation spot of Campbell and his wife, Anne. He didn't race until he was four years old in 1989, starting six times, mostly at Turfway Park, and finishing second twice. As a five-year-old he raced only twice, in early 1990, breaking his maiden in the very last race of his career, an 8½-furlong maiden claiming race, also at Turfway Park.

"He was a very average racehorse, and Mr. Campbell did not want claiming horses," said trainer Phil Simms. "He decided to retire him and see if the horse could find another career instead."

Simms said he remembered Banyan House because he was so agreeable.

"He was a laid-back, strong, and solid horse," he said. "He was a sweetheart."

When I tracked down Campbell, he laughed when I mentioned Banyan House, saying he recalled him because the colt took so long to get to the track. Whereas most of Campbell's horses are coming off the track at age four, Banyan House wasn't ready to race until he was four, and even then he didn't show much but an affable temperament.

He doesn't remember to whom he gave Banyan House when he retired him, but Midway College certainly wouldn't be out of the question. "I love all of my horses, and I try to find good homes for them," he said.

Today, Banion is the lone horse used at Riding for Hope for non-mounted therapy, excepting the minis, of course. He primarily is used to help clients work through mental health issues. Someone facing tough times may discover the healing value of sharing her struggle through an exercise in which she uses a lead rope to navigate Banion through an obstacle course. Along the way, she must pick up and carry objects, including a big plastic yellow peanut about the size of two large pillows. As the objects, particularly the peanut, weigh her down, she finds it impossible to carry everything and lead Banion. The second time through the course, a surcingle is placed around Banion body and she attaches the peanut, making it easier for her to pick up objects and navigate the obstacles.

"It's a metaphor to ask for help to get through life's hard times," said Spittler.

One day, she said, a group of teenage girls came to Riding for Hope as part of a counseling and team-building session. After one activity, they gathered in a circle with a counselor for a post mortem. When the talk turned heavy, one girl began to cry, walking away for a little privacy. Banion followed the girl and stood right next to her until she had calmed down and was ready to rejoin the group.

"He meets people where they are," Spittler told me.

Thankfully, he had someone to meet him when his career on the racetrack ended. I can only hope the same for Hurry to Flag.

Race and (Stakes) Record						
YEAR	AGE	STS	1ST	2ND	3RD	EARNED
1989	at 4	6	0 (0)	2 (0)	0 (0)	$2,035
1990	at 5	2	1 (0)	0 (0)	0 (0)	$3,570
Lifetime		8	1 (0)	2 (0)	0 (0)	$5,605

BUCKINGHAM PLACE

By ALICIA WINCZE

T here was no international glory on the line
or high-profile national team selections at
stake — just a preliminary eventing competition, held in Aiken,
South Carolina, in February 2008.

2

Still, as Tara Ziegler looked at the judges' comments following
that day's dressage test aboard her then thirteen-year-old gelding
Buckingham Place, she knew she had become part of something
special. "He got the comment at the bottom of the test that said
'Happy horse,' " Tara recalled. "And the other comments were
'fluid and relaxed.' I was mad at him because he had stopped (at a
jump), but then I got my dressage test back, and I was like 'Wow.
Is this the same horse?' "

Truth is, Buckingham Place hasn't been the same horse for some
time now.

In the demanding sport of eventing — the three-phase competition comprising dressage, cross-country, and show jumping
— there is no higher competitive level than the four-star ech-
elon. During the 2007 and 2008 seasons Tara and Buckingham
Place found themselves in that tier, competing alongside the leg-

ends of their game at the prestigious Rolex Kentucky Three-Day Event held each April at the Kentucky Horse Park in Lexington, Kentucky.

That Ziegler's 16-hand dark bay Thoroughbred would go jump-for-jump with some of the most accomplished event horses in the world hardly seemed possible when he labored on the backstretch of Penn National Race Course in Grantville, Pennsylvania, just seven years earlier. For the first six years of his life, Buckingham Place was a racehorse, a bottom-level claimer who made forty career starts and visited the winner's circle only four times.

Although he was bred in Kentucky by small-time owner Dr. Robert Fishman, his pedigree was only modestly better than his race record. Buckingham Place is by the respected stallion Buckaroo, who had sired a Horse of the Year in Spend a Buck, but his dam, Old Maid, was an undistinguished broodmare as she failed to produce a single stakes winner from nine offspring.

Eight years ago, however, Tara and her mother Kim, who operates a ten-acre training and sales facility at Lincoln University in Pennsylvania, were checking out potential eventing prospects at the local track when they stumbled upon the quirky gelding. While his physical attributes were obvious, so too was the fact he was in desperate need of a career change.

It was the eighth race of the day on the Penn National card on March 2, 2001. A slight-looking entrant named Buckingham Place stepped into the starting gate attempting to halt a fifteen-race losing streak that stretched back to April of the previous year.

With jockey Ricardo Cannon aboard, the gelding advanced to fourth in the seven-horse field but then faded badly as he entered the stretch of the 1¹⁄₁₆-mile race, coming home next to last while beaten 13¾ lengths.

Before his handlers could even get him cooled out, the droplets of blood trickling from his flared nostrils told them why his latest effort had resulted in just another in a long line of busts. For the third time in his career, the edgy gelding had bled through his Lasix — the diuretic drug used to treat pulmonary hemorrhaging in racehorses — and with that, his chances of ever going back to the track were over.

"He was kind of a nervous horse and he was a bad bleeder, which can go hand in hand with nervous horses," said Marcia Wolfe, whose husband Robert Wolfe Jr. claimed Buckingham Place for Mr. and Mrs. John Berry in October 1999 and trained the gelding for the remainder of his career. "What I remember best about him, though, is years ago, when the track went on strike, we shipped the horses over to a farm and turned everyone out for a couple hours a day, and one day he decided he didn't want to get caught.

"It was the dead of winter and we didn't want to leave him out there so we got a couple people to corral him into the corner of the fence and, don't you know, he went right up and over it. So in a way, that was his future. That was his destiny because he's surely found his calling now."

While fate is not always kind to lower-level racehorses whose careers come to undistinguished ends, Buckingham Place did not have to wait long for a more promising future. A day after the gelding had bled, Kim and Tara made their way out to Penn National on the referral of a friend, hoping to find a couple of sound prospects to be retrained as event horses and eventually resold.

For years Kim had been scouring the tracks for mentally and physically sound racehorses no longer at the top of their game. While the backside of a modest racetrack may not seem like the ideal place to discover the next four-star protégé, Kim knew any horse that could successfully endure exhausting morning workouts and battle a field of race foes before a roaring crowd would have a better-than-average chance of standing up to the rigors of eventing. She also discovered that the quality of horse she can find there is high for the small price she pays to relieve an owner of an unwanted Thoroughbred.

When none of the initial horses at Penn National resonated with the Zieglers, Marcia Wolfe directed their attention toward the gelding in her care that had bled the night before and now needed to be sold. Despite his light frame and average look, Buckingham Place won over the Zieglers with his ample walk and solid conformation. "They led him out of his stall and he was kind of lightly built, but he overstepped by about a foot at the walk and had this real nice swing to his gait," Kim said. "He was really correct — and Tara loved him, so that pretty much did it. I think we went back the next day with the checkbook and got him for about $1,200."

After giving their new charge a brief period of down time to adjust to life away from the racetrack, the Zieglers began the process of retraining Buckingham Place, which included teaching him to adjust to different, more subtle signals coming from the rider and getting him out of the mindset that his only mission in life was to go as fast as he could for as long as he could.

Physically, he had all the necessary tools to make the transition into an event horse because he had remained remarkably sound throughout his forty-race career. Trying to get Buckingham Place to overcome the mental issues he had racked up, however, proved nearly as daunting as a cross-country ride.

Although good natured in his overall temperament, the gelding remained on edge mentally, spooking at even the most natural of things around the farm. Ample work on the ground and idyllic trail rides helped relax his mind, but it was years before Buckingham Place was able to adapt to change without any adverse affects.

"I think the track just really stressed him out," said twenty-five-year-old Tara, who graduated from Lincoln University in May 2006. "I think some horses can handle it, but it just stressed him out and was overwhelming for him. He's had focus problems and ... he would get stressed out when we took him places and he never wanted to eat. You couldn't put anything in his food or else he wouldn't eat it. I'd say it was almost three years before we could totally get him flushed out to where he was really happy and healthy eating-wise."

The original plan called for Buckingham Place to be one of Kim's sales projects. But once again the gelding's future took an unexpected turn.

Kim had heard the tale of Buckingham Place's agile paddock escape while he was turned out during the Penn National track strike, so she figured he would have no problem clearing a set of railroad ties she had set up at the farm.

To Kim's dismay, however, when she attempted to jump her new project over the modest-sized ties, the sound of his legs whacking each and every one made her wonder if a career dependent upon clearing obstacles was really the best path for him after all.

"The ties are only about so big, but for some reason he just nailed them three times in a row really hard," Tara said with a laugh. "After that, my mom was like 'Here, see what you can do with him.'"

The dressage portion of eventing wasn't always his strong suit.

It had been Tara, after all, who was most impressed with what she saw emerge from the stall at Penn National weeks earlier, so taking on Buckingham Place was a challenge she would not turn down.

As part of the training, Tara brought her new mount over for a lesson with her coach, Olympic gold medalist Phillip Dutton. Not only did Dutton confirm there was indeed true potential within Buckingham Place's smallish frame, he suggested that Tara and her mother had gotten a much better deal than they initially believed.

"I brought him over there when I was going about training, and he had a line set up with poles in the middle and Buck jumped every pole all the way through — just ping-ping-ping," Tara said. "Phillip said, 'Don't tell your mom, but this one might be worth some money.' And if Phillip likes him, I figured I should keep him. Of course, once I get a hold of them, I never want to sell any of them."

With his inherent jumping ability and his residual speed and stamina from his time on the track, Buckingham Place began morphing into a careful, scopey performer in both the cross-country and stadium jumping portions of eventing. However, getting his dressage up to speed proved to be an albatross that would hang over horse and rider for years.

The precise movements and seamless transitions involved with dressage make it as much a mental challenge as it is a physical one. It was not uncommon for a battle of wills to break out between Tara and her gelding while in the ring.

Direct cues from Tara's seat and leg were often evaded. Shoulders were popped the opposite way. When Buckingham Place did execute what was asked of him, it usually was on his terms.

"I'm kind of a pushover," Tara said. "I'm not the strictest. I'm not always the most particular person. I'm happy to get what I'm asking for a moment and then move on, which doesn't always cut it when you're trying to get a whole test that is decent. So it's a learning process for both of us."

"He's a nice mover and has all the right ingredients, but mentally he's a bit tight," Kim added. "A lot of people may not have spent that much time on him but all credit to Tara. She kind of hung in there because he was never easy."

Much of Tara's persistence comes from the fact she has been on horseback "since I was in the womb," she proclaims, as her mother has been competing and training event horses for more than thirty years.

Having been given her first pony at the age of three, Tara showed she inherited her mother's natural ability and touch in the saddle when she was selected to compete on her first Young

Buckingham Place relishes galloping during the cross-country phase.

Riders team — a program specifically intended to prepare riders twenty-one years of age and younger for international competition — in 2001 before competing on the two-star squad in 2003.

The experience of learning what it took to compete at a top level helped Tara realize she was picking up her own bad habits to compensate for Buckingham Place's shortcomings. Thus, Tara found by riding more seasoned horses along the way she could get a better feel for the proper techniques to help correct his weak points.

"He's really hard to get straight and so he's gotten me in the habit to correct his evasions that aren't correct," Tara said. "By riding other horses that are more correct and that go straighter naturally I've been able to go 'Oh, I need to be using this rein more properly' and that will help his evasion instead of just doing things I thought were a quick fix."

By 2005 Tara and Buckingham Place were regulars at the intermediate level and earned their first victory in the Young Rider open intermediate division of the Surefire Farm Horse Trials in Purcellville, Virginia, that July.

In October 2005, the duo competed in their first two-star event together at Radnor Hunt in Malvern, Pennsylvania, finishing a respectable ninth in a field that included such accomplished participants as her coach Dutton and Olympian Karen O'Connor.

After successfully completing their first three-star event at Fair Hill in Maryland in October 2006, finishing twenty-fourth out of more than forty riders, Tara decided to find out what they were truly capable of and entered the 2007 Rolex Kentucky Three-Day Event on the final day applications were due.

"I didn't really tell my mom because she didn't think I was ready for it," Tara said. "I figured if I got there and the cross-country course looks like we can't handle it, we won't go.

"But I got there and walked the course and there was nothing here he hasn't seen in some way, shape, or form. It was maybe a little bigger and all together it's a lot harder, but I thought 'I think we can do it,' and we did. We made it around. I thought the experience was good for both of us."

Tara's biggest concern was having her flighty gelding melt down in front of a crowd much larger than he was accustomed to. But while his tension issues resulted in a penalty score of 78.5 in the dressage phase, Buckingham Place was able to grit his way around the cross-country course and knocked down just one rail during the show jumping portion as the duo finished twenty-seventh, ahead of Olympians Bruce Davidson, Becky Holder, and Amy Tryon.

"Some people thought Tara shouldn't even be there — and honestly I was right there with them," Kim said. "But she completed it and had a little better result than was expected. That was definitely the highest point so far."

Tara is quick to point out the learning process is still ongoing between herself and Buckingham Place, and their bad days sometimes outnumber the good.

At the 2008 Rolex Kentucky Three-Day Event, an unfocused Buckingham Place again squirmed his way through the dressage test, but the pair was eliminated in the cross-country phase after Tara fell at fence sixteen and then failed to clear the "B" element of the fence after remounting.

"We've had some really nice moments. Our show jumping now

Tara and Buckingham Place competed at the Kentucky-Rolex Three-Day Event.

is more a function of me than him because he really is a good jumper," Tara said. "He doesn't like to touch the rails, but again his focus can be the problem. I'm still waiting for the moment where he goes into an awards ceremony and stands quietly, but he continues to keep growing up."

His stall door isn't always draped with blue ribbons, but when Tara looks at Buckingham Place these days, she sees a far more rewarding picture. The bleeding that plagued the gelding during his time on the track has never returned and although Tara has some

29

young prospects she is working with, he now ranks as the primary horse she competes with at the advanced level.

While Buckingham Place still has a penchant for acting like an inexperienced youngster when approaching a new fence for the first time, such issues are now momentary annoyances rather than long-term struggles.

The one thing that has become readily apparent to all who come in contact with the unlikely duo, however, is that Tara now has a fit, happy companion with whom she loves to work.

"I love the fact that he is a completely different horse than he was when I got him," she said. "He's happy and he likes his job. He still has his tendencies, but he's more mature, laid back. He's so much easier now that sometimes I forget just how much he has changed."

Race and (Stakes) Record						
YEAR	AGE	STS	1ST	2ND	3RD	EARNED
1998	at 3	8	0 (0)	0 (0)	1 (0)	$2,650
1999	at 4	14	2 (0)	1 (0)	1 (0)	$9,405
2000	at 5	14	2 (0)	2 (0)	1 (0)	$10,393
2001	at 6	4	0 (0)	0 (0)	1 (0)	$850
Lifetime		**40**	**4 (0)**	**3 (0)**	**4 (0)**	**$23,298**

(A version of this chapter appeared previously in the Lexington [Kentucky] Herald-Leader.)

Congomambo

By Katie Merwick

3

On a pitch black, bitterly cold November evening Carrie McCarthy was just leaving the boarding stable where she kept her horse when she heard the rumble of a stock trailer rolling down the gravel driveway. A squeal of brakes cracked the icy stillness as the truck strained to a halt.

Carrie recognized the trailer. It belonged to the stable owner. In addition to offering a self-care arrangement for other people to board their horses, he operated a hack (horse rental) business from the barn. Carrie, the thirty-year-old daughter of Pennsylvania racehorse trainer Bill McCarthy, wished all the horses at the stable received the same love, care, and respect as she gave her own, but this was not the case. She sat in her car for a moment, wondering if she dared to see what unfortunate horses were being brought in this time. But it was late, and she decided to continue home.

She glanced at the trailer in her rear view mirror as she slowly drove away, the glare from its red taillights dimming.

The driver yanked the rusty door open and a tall, lanky Thoroughbred gelding stumbled out of the stock trailer. He trembled as the door of the empty trailer slammed shut behind him but was too exhausted to react any more than that. The Coggins health report read that he was a "grade" horse, meaning he was in such bad condition that he couldn't be identified as a Thoroughbred, and was estimated to be between ten and twelve years old.

A teenaged girl who worked for the stable led the gelding into his new home. It was an old cow barn, dank and musty, constructed of stone and mapped out like a maze with the horses stabled below ground level. The ceilings underground were low and caked with thick cobwebs. The gelding was forced to walk with his head awkwardly low to avoid hitting the ceiling. The slow and carefully placed clank of his metal shoes on the cement floor echoed as he walked. They arrived at an isolated straight stall in the very back of the barn. It resembled a bay such as you would find in a straight-load horse trailer in which the horse has enough room to stand comfortably but not enough room to turn around. As no natural light could come in, and most of the light bulbs had burned out, only an outline of the horse's large frame inside the stall could be seen. The girl named the new horse "Tornado," but as English was not her first language, she was not able to pronounce it correctly. Instead, his name at the barn became "Tomato."

The stable owner had purchased the horse for $325 out of a kill pen at a nearby sale in Camelot, New Jersey. However, his fate as a neglected hack horse was nearly as grim as the slaughterhouse. A no-win situation.

Days passed while the despondent gelding stood quietly in the straight stall, his head tied to the wall so that he could not back out. It seemed as if he had accepted his fate at the rental stables. Eventually, the girl returned to let Tomato out of his stall. Hobbling obediently on swollen legs behind her to the turnout paddock, he gulped in the fresh air. Before his eyes could adjust to daylight, one of the rental horses in the same paddock kicked him in the hock. Tomato was returned to his stall that afternoon and again tied to the wall. His injured hock went unnoticed for several days as the owner did not provide much more than minimal care — enough food and water for survival.

When Carrie returned to the stables to tend to her ten-year-old Paint horse, Chief, she brought along her friend, Pam Shavelson, a racehorse trainer. They happened to take a different route through the barn to Chief's stall, passing through a dimly lit hallway and down a small ramp toward the underground stalls. The low ceilings and stale air were almost suffocating. Carrie zipped her coat up all the way, fending off the dampness. Their voices echoed off the stone walls in the stillness of the empty barn. They had reached the very back of the barn where most people do not frequent, and where no other horses were kept at the time.

As the two women stepped around a corner and approached the stall where Tomato was confined, Carrie heard a soft nicker. The sound of helplessness in that call stopped her dead in her tracks.

She wondered what a horse was doing all the way back here, alone. Her intuition told her it must be the horse that had arrived on the trailer earlier in the week. Carrie peered into the gloomy stall, afraid of what she would see. A tall, painfully thin gelding stretched his head around as far as his rope would allow and made eye contact with Carrie.

The stench of urine, manure, and rotting moldy hay nearly made her gag. Without questioning their instincts, Carrie and Pam

The imbedded halter left a permanent scar on Congomambo's face.

backed Tomato out of the straight stall and put him in a cross-tie to examine him.

The horse was 400 pounds underweight, and his winter coat was three inches long, making him look more like a woolly mammoth than a horse. His fetlocks were swollen. He wore a nylon halter several sizes too small; it had been left on for so long it had rubbed him raw. The skin had healed over the halter, embedding the strap into his face. Carrie's first reaction was "Oh my God, you poor thing! What happened to you?" She noticed many things that needed immediate attention such as the infected wound on his face and the untreated hock injury.

Compelled to help, Carrie retrieved her emergency veterinary kit, which had all the basic tools for minor injuries and illnesses. Over the years Carrie had assisted her father in treating the injuries of their racehorses and had learned always to be prepared. She and Pam began by removing the nylon halter, which had to be cut and pulled out from under his skin, creating a gash that ran three-quarters of the way down the side of his face. "He was a class act," Carrie remembered. "You could tell he was fearful of people, but he stood there stoic and brave. He didn't attempt to kick or bite even with a painful condition — he was just grateful that someone finally took notice of the injuries he had."

Carrie and Pam cleaned his face wound with a surgical scrub and slathered it with a soothing antibiotic ointment. They iced down his hot, swollen hock with cold water and applied a leg wrap to keep pressure on the swelling until they could give him an oral medication for inflammation.

Pam had cleaned out the stall and filled it with the little bit of clean shavings she could find. She scrubbed the slime from his water bucket and rinsed it until it smelled fresh again. When they had done all they could that night, Carrie tucked him back into his stall with plenty of clean water and several flakes of fresh hay from her own supply. She left his halter off and his head untied. Carrie and Pam both vowed, out loud, that they would be back.

The next day Carrie and Pam approached the stable owner, asking for permission to rehabilitate the horse. It made no difference to him and, ungratefully, he agreed.

Tomato was dewormed and vaccinated, and his diet was supplemented with high-calorie feed and vitamins. His hooves were trimmed and reshaped so that he could walk with ease. The more time the girls spent with Tomato, the more attached they became to him. Pam committed to a two-month lease on Tomato, which was all she could afford at the time. They had already invested a substantial amount of time and money into his rehabilitation, but to see the change in his mental and physical well-being made it all worthwhile.

Having the lease in place allowed Carrie and Pam to take Tomato out for fresh air on the trails. Although Pam trained racehorses, she had not ridden a horse in thirty years. Tomato took on the role of babysitter and took care of her, building her confidence in riding again. They rode on the trails in a group, Carrie on Chief and Pam on Tomato.

As the months passed, with good nutrition and care Tomato's once lackluster, coarse coat shed out. Pam lovingly nicknamed him "the yak boy" because of his long, thinning hair. Washed and groomed, Tomato's new coat glistened and his silky mane was trimmed and tidy. A soft look replaced the dread in his eye. "It's funny," Carrie explained, "down the road, once he started feeling better, more of his personality came out."

Many Thoroughbreds are thin-skinned or sensitive to grooming. Carrie laughed as she recalled how Tomato transformed from stoic gentleman to reactive drama king over simple grooming or medicating tasks. He would bite at the stall door, the feed bucket, anything in front of him when being curried but never acted out toward people. Even rubbing soothing ointment onto a cut turned Tomato into a nervous wreck. "After being so brave through all of that painful rehabilitation, now he's a big baby!" said Carrie.

The most challenging behavior to work through was gaining his trust and working around his head. "He would give you that look with fear in his eye. To this day he is very weird about his ears and the side of his face that was injured," said Carrie. "I think someone must have twitched his ears."

When Pam could no longer afford to lease Tomato, the owner announced that he would put him out on the hack line, available for anyone to rent. Carrie knew all of the progress that had been made both physically and mentally would vanish. The weight he had gained would disappear. Often, Carrie had observed inexperienced rental riders beat the horses and overwork them into exhaustion. Carrie was not willing to betray the horse that had found it in his heart to trust a human after all of the injustice he had endured. This horse had the dignity restored to his life, and he returned her love tenfold. Carrie remembers, "Tomato was very selective about who he trusted, and still is to this day. No one working for the hack stables would ever have earned or deserved his trust."

The owner wanted $1,500 cash for Tomato, apparently not taking into consideration all of the time, expenses, and leasing fees that Carrie and Pam had already invested. So be it. Carrie ponied up the money, and Tomato was hers.

That very day Carrie moved Tomato to a more reputable farm down the street. It was more than she could afford, long term, but for now she wanted to remove Tomato from any association with the previous owner. The new barn gave him impeccable care, sweet-smelling clean bedding in his stall, groomed paddocks and pasture, abundant fresh food, and clean water. Surrounded by happy, well-adjusted horses that welcomed him into the herd, he blossomed and slowly regained the magnificent conformation he once had, a full-bodied 16.3-hand beauty.

Ultimately, Carrie hoped to find Tomato the perfect, permanent home. Until then, he would remain safe in her care. "I knew I couldn't afford both Chief and Tomato long term, but we don't always choose when horses come into our lives or when they leave. I would never let anything happen to Tomato."

A slew of people looked at him, but nobody took him home. He was too green for one, too small for another, and too tall for yet another. Several people who did want him didn't pass Carrie's screening process. It was important to make sure the next owner would have suitable stabling and the knowledge to care for and continue training Tomato.

After several months Carrie decided to board Tomato once again at the stables he originally came from. It was less expensive and she felt he would have better exposure for adoption. This time, however, Tomato's stall was near Chief's, in a larger, well-lighted space with good ventilation.

With each day that passed Tomato became more adoptable and social. Convinced that his "person" was out there, Carrie believed it was only a matter of time and patience before the right person would come along.

The most frequently asked question from prospective owners was about Tomato's pedigree. Naturally curious, Carrie and Pam had tried to decipher his lip tattoo earlier in the year. The first letter and last number, however, were barely legible. Carrie's friend, Niki Yaeger, happened to work in the office of the Philadelphia Park racetrack. She gave officials the horse's age and the numbers that could be deciphered. They discovered two horses he might be.

Patient nursing by Carrie and Pam returned Congomambo to health.

Both had raced in New Mexico and Arizona as three-year-olds and were now eleven years old.

But there was something extraordinary about this horse. Something majestic. Something inexplicable that begged for an answer. Carrie was not convinced that Tomato was either of the horses their research had revealed. After reading an article about how using a flashlight in a dark area can help bring out the ink of a horse's tattoo, she decided to give it a try. To her amazement, it worked. Carrie was able to decipher the previously indiscernible first letter, C, and last number, 2, to complete the tattoo.

Carrie immediately contacted The Jockey Club to discover the true identity of Tomato. What happened next took her breath away.

Rather than being eleven years old, he was only six. Although his age was much younger than Carrie and Pam had suspected, his blue-blooded pedigree was not surprising. Having been raised in a home of racehorse trainers, Carrie had an eye for horses. Everyone who met this horse knew there had to be more to his story.

Tomato's real name was Congomambo, a son of the excellent racehorse and sire Kingmambo, (who has stood at stud for as much as $300,000) out of the mare Lubicon (the 1990 champion three-year-old filly in Canada). Foaled in 1999, Congomambo was bred in Kentucky by Live Oak Plantation, a Florida-based Thoroughbred operation owned by Charlotte Weber, the heir to the Campbell Soup fortune.

How did such a regally bred horse, whose sire's colts have sold for more than $1 million at sales, end up in a slaughter pen? There were holes in the timeline that needed explanation.

Eager to fill in all the blanks, Carrie pulled Congomambo's entire race record to find that Live Oak did not enter him in the yearling sale but instead kept and raced him. His first race was as a three-year-old at Gulfstream Park in Florida. His second and third races that same year were at Belmont Park in New York. He was injured in his third start, a maiden special weight, given nine months off, and then brought back to race in Florida. He was not consistent as a racehorse, not the type of horse that Live Oak kept in its stable, so the owners sold him to their trainer, William Cesare, in 2003.

Congomambo won a few races for Cesare, but the horse's stamina deteriorated. After running poorly for $8,000 at Calder, he was sold to the Henry Worcester outfit that competes at Charlestown in West Virginia. He ran a few times for $5,000 and won for $3,500.

His last race came on May 13, 2005 — a $3,500 claiming race in which he finished a bad fifth.

Congomambo had raced far longer than he should have and had given more than anyone should have asked. At the age of six with thirty-five starts, his ankles were locked and he had very limited mobility. However, racing was in his blood. He willingly gave all that he could. The individual with the Henry Worchester outfit who owned him had planned to take him to Florida and send him to a retirement farm, but that plan never came to fruition. Somewhere between that last race in May 2005 and November 2005, he was dumped at a kill pen in New Jersey. Fortunately, death at the slaughterhouse was not his destiny.

Carrie wrote to Charlotte Weber to inform her of Congomambo's present circumstances. Soon after, she received a written reply. The Webers were, of course, appalled by what had happened to Congomambo and grateful to Carrie for finding him a suitable home. They graciously offered to welcome him back if ever he needed a home, but Carrie and the horse she had learned to love as Tomato had come so far together and their journey was not yet complete.

In May 2008 Tomato began the final chapter of his life. Carrie heard that Jaime McKeehan and her mother, whom she knew through the equestrian community, had purchased their own farm. She knew this family would give Tomato a very safe, comfortable, and loving permanent home.

Jaime was not actively shopping for a horse at the time Carrie approached her about Tomato. Isn't that when it always happens? When you least expect it?

Jaime and Congomambo quickly developed a bond.

Jaime had grown up riding her now twenty-one-year-old Paint gelding, Cowboy. When she drifted away from horses in high school and college, Cowboy became her mother's mount. Now interested in riding again, Jaime had been passively looking for the perfect horse.

Reluctantly, Jaime came to the barn to meet Tomato. She had never considered owning a Thoroughbred. "The first thing I noticed about him was his size," recalled Jaime. "In the stall he looked huge compared to my other horse (Cowboy) and other horses I had ridden."

Carrie walked Tomato out of the barn on a lead line — he towered over her. Jaime observed Tomato walking quietly, and yet he was very aware of his surroundings as they headed for the riding arena. Shimmering in the sunlight, his sleek spring coat showed off his muscular frame.

Jaime was apprehensive about her first ride, as she had not ridden consistently in years. Once she had mounted, Tomato's height and large, round belly were a bit intimidating. She sat quietly at first, digging deep for confidence.

"I could tell he was a solid horse by the way he stood so still when I got up," she recalled.

Tomato waited patiently. It did not take long for her to trust him. "I never felt that he would run off with me or hurt me."

Soon, Jaime felt a connection with Tomato, the kind of connection where there is clear communication between horse and rider. He performed as if he knew he was interviewing for the most important job of his life. It seemed he was truly doing his best to do whatever Jaime asked. He had stolen her heart.

Cowboy and Congomambo became fast friends and pasturemates.

Carrie gave Tomato to Jaime with the agreement that if for any reason she could not keep him, he would be returned to Carrie. On May 1, 2008, Jaime brought Tomato home, turning him out with Cowboy. The new friends bonded immediately.

Carrie returned to visit Tomato after he had settled in. There was a special spot in her heart for this horse she had nursed back from despondency. Carrie knew her role in his life was simply to help him find his way to a good home. Mesmerized by his noble spirit, Carrie and Jaime watched Tomato gallop with powerful strides through the pasture. They imagined him in his prime — the rush of adrenalin, splashing mud, and pounding hooves — as he thundered down the racetrack. Tomato once again carried himself with confidence. Knowing some of what he had endured, Carrie and Jaime understood why he seemed so grateful for every bit of kindness.

Race and (Stakes) Record

YEAR	AGE	STS	1ST	2ND	3RD	EARNED
2002	at 3	3	0 (0)	1 (0)	0 (0)	$9,120
2003	at 4	12	1 (0)	0 (0)	2 (0)	$13,160
2004	at 5	14	1 (0)	2 (0)	2 (0)	$12,470
2005	at 6	6	1 (0)	0 (0)	0 (0)	$5,335
Lifetime		**35**	**3 (0)**	**3 (0)**	**4 (0)**	**$40,115**

DECLAN'S MOON

BY JOSH PONS

4

Believe in the coming of one good horse. The next mare, the next foal, the next yearling, the next stallion, the next walk up that hill. Could be the horse you're looking for. Just listen to this unlikely story.

As I lift the microphone from its keeper on the karaoke machine, I look up the driveway to make sure the good horse is out of earshot: "Testing. Testing. One, two."

A hundred horse racing fans are having lunch on the lawn at Merryland Farm, a gracious old training facility in a beautiful long green valley of Maryland. They are gathered here today for a fall picnic. To be excited by horses and country air, out of offices and off the crawling commute, if only for these few hours. And to see a star racehorse.

Just the proximity to the white rails of the racetrack sparks an adrenaline rush in the crowd. Like holding a meeting in a billiard hall. Something fun happens here. We will soon be parading sets of freshly broken yearlings, pairs of breezing two-year-olds, an occasional older horse coming off a lay-up. But first ...

"Welcome to our annual Autumn Day in the Country."

Guests look up from bowls of crab soup. Stiff with stage-fright, I hear my voice echo out of the song machine.

"This year we have a special guest, Declan's Moon, Eclipse Award winner and champion two-year-old of 2004."

Up the lane, Declan's Moon bends his long neck and stares down his nose at the wide wooden bridge, absorbing the light, calculating the risk, his groom, Maurilio, giving him enough shank, enough time. It's a moment of concentration I've seen before, in newsreel footage of post parades as he swept those big stakes races in California, the racing channels avidly following a two-year-old Kentucky Derby hopeful.

Those four races when he was two. The surprise Del Mar debut at 15-1. The stretch-long battle with Roman Ruler in the Del Mar Futurity. The gallop in the Hollywood Preview. The wire-to-wire win in the Hollywood Futurity at Christmas, against Breeders' Cup victor Wilko, eventual Kentucky Derby winner Giacomo, and Champagne Stakes winner Proud Accolade, the track announcer wildly proclaiming that "Declan's Moon is a total eclipse." A play on the bronze horse, the Eclipse Award, all his at the finish line. Year-end voting a mere formality for the undefeated Maryland-bred. Four-for-four. The Derby the goal.

We've been around Declan for six weeks now, since his arrival in early August. So territorial at first. Like a stallion. But Declan is a gelding. Day by day, he has transitioned from spoiled star to regular guy. He stands 16.1 hands, with knowing eyes set in a fine head. He exudes star power. We trust him to behave during today's show, but take no chances. A second groom, Fabian, walks a short distance behind Maurilio. Declan's eyes roll back and spot the backup groom. He gets the message.

Declans Moon winning the Hollywood Futurity over Giacomo

Now he steps forward onto the bridge and crosses above the fresh-flowing creek coursing through the farm. His ankles, all four, are spackled with white hairs, but his hooves are mostly black. Good hard feet. His white ankles flash with every step, like Fred Astaire in white socks. I begin speaking before he gets closer, so he won't be startled as he nears the microphone.

"This is the first time Declan's Moon has been led across the bridge. I ask you all to please be quiet while he's down here. He doesn't quite know what's expected of him today."

Declan is in full elegant walk on the driveway, an engaged stride, almost a jog on the end of Maurilio's leather shank. The folks on the lawn sit behind a low privet hedge. Many of them stand now, to gain a better view. Their rising becomes a silent ovation. Declan returns their gaze. Swaggers like a dressage horse. Confident. Intelligent. He is making converts in the crowd. Laity suddenly aware of a spirit. He has presence, as they say. He certainly has presence.

Suddenly, Declan spots the white rails of the track. His walk becomes more aggressive, stronger, purposeful. He wants to drag Maurilio over to the track. He wants the feel of sand under his feet. Maurilio speaks to him.

"No. No. Not today, Declan."

Fabian scurries to the entrance gap. Slides out a recessed length of rail to close off the opening. I watch this little scene as I continue.

"No one knows where a good horse will come from. You could say Declan came out of an ad in the local paper."

I shorthand through oral history for the crowd. Imagine this beginning. Maryland cattleman Brice Ridgely spooning down Sunday breakfast on a brisk February morning ten years ago in the kitchen of his farm in Cooksville. Calloused hands creasing the classifieds. Reading glasses small as a bird on a bull's back. Scans the columns.

"How 'bout this? Thoroughbred mare Fabulous Vee. Twelve-year-old stakes producer."

He dials the number. Sets up a time to see the mare. His wife, Mary Anne, knows his big heart, rides shotgun. She grew up on a storybook farm chopped off the mainland by Interstate 70. She's usually not sentimental. She's a farm girl who knows how a horse should look. Sees the mare's yearling in the barn, a leggy bay filly by a young stud named Norquestor. A little light in flesh. Filly

Declan's Moon striking a pose in his paddock at Country Life Farm

would quickly fit up on some of Brice's homegrown hay and his fresh-milled sweet feed.

"You can't take the mare unless you buy her yearling too," Mary Anne tells Brice.

A package deal is struck: $3,500 for mother and daughter. Not for one second do they think they are buying the dam of a future champion, but they know it could happen. See, that's the mystery at the heart of the horse business: No one knows where a good horse will come from.

Declan's Moon stands behind me, frozen for his fans. They have edged closer to the low hedge. He could be posing for a conformation photo. Digital cameras click. Folks squint through viewfinders of cell-phone cameras. He's a movie star. He's a male model. He's beautiful and he knows it in that natural way wild animals show pride. He's the best horse many of these folks have ever seen up close, in person. As he holds the pose, I think about the comment made by my wife Ellen.

"He looks like one of those racehorses from old paintings. All legs. High headed."

I see that now. An eighteenth-century sportsman, a duke, an earl, would certainly have commissioned a portrait by Stull, Herring, Stubbs, Marshall. To capture Declan's great expressive eyes, his exaggerated gait, that serpentine neck, straight out of the era when racehorses were painted with all four feet off the ground; front legs reaching, hind legs sprung out behind, nothing but air underneath.

At standstill, Declan could have posed for the Eclipse Award, the bronze likeness of Stubbs' iconic portrait of unbeaten Eclipse, held at the corner of the brick bathhouse at Newmarket, saddled up, ears pinned, eyes anxious, mouth slightly opened. Eclipse.

Declan's black coat is dappled in circles of health, but the first thick hairs brought on by cool nights dull the sheen, winter coat roughing in. He carries weight over his ribs, but snapshots taken today reveal that in-between period, not yet let down from racing, not built up from pasture. Finally, he moves out of his pose, drawn again toward the white rails of the track. Maurilio tightens his hold as the horse's eyes fix with the preoccupied look of a gladiator. Maurilio doesn't tempt fate. Turns the horse in a wide circle.

"Declan. This way. This way."

Maurilio circles Declan again, and again.

Brice was a young bid-spotter for Fasig-Tipton back when the Saratoga yearling sales ran for four hard nights that stretched into early mornings. He went into the auction business for himself. Became the last call for retiring farmers, once their offspring got a taste of nine-to-five suburban life, eight-hour days, weekends off.

"Get what you can, Brice. That's my life you're selling there."

Brice auctioned their tractors, hay wagons, anything not tied down.

So knowledgeable about value, he thought nothing of buying horses out of the classifieds. Fabulous Vee and her yearling filly came home to Spring Meadow, the Ridgely family farm on busy Route 97. Too close to Washington, D.C., and Baltimore to remain unspoiled. An incongruous franchised convenience store flanks the front of Spring Meadow. It is the twentieth-century version of a general store, where everybody knows your name, where Brice buys diesel fuel for trailer rides up I-95 to Maryland stallion farms.

The leggy yearling, they named Vee Vee Star. She raced in Mary Anne's silks, won twice, covered expenses with $60,895 in purses. Earned a home in the broodmare band when, as longshot local in the famous Black-Eyed Susan Stakes at Pimlico, she cantered home third behind Hall of Famer Silverbulletday. Grade II black type for Timonium catalog pages.

Brice watched Malibu Moon, a three-year-old son of A. P. Indy, servicing mares at Country Life Farm. Injured after winning one race at two.

"Any stud bred at three ever amount to anything?"

"Raise a Native. Hail to Reason."

"Send me a contract."

He trailered Vee Vee Star up I-95 in Malibu Moon's second season. Delivered the resulting foal on February 20, 2002. Named the baby for his grandson Declan. Fed him the best homegrown Howard County hay a farmer can raise. Castrated him as a yearling because he was heavy as a bull and because that's what real farmers do with livestock of modest description, like what you find in classifieds.

"Saves the next fellow from the expense," Brice explained, code of courtesy handed down from farming ancestors. He showed Declan's Moon to longtime friend and sales agent Bill Reightler.

"Start sale-prepping this colt now, Brice. Walk some of that fat off him."

"That's muscle!"

"He looks like a steer ready for market."

"That's how I raise 'em!"

He entered Declan's Moon in the October yearling sale. Kept him out of the summer sun. Had him ready when Malibu Moon's first crop came out running. Perfect Moon, a $4,700 Timonium yearling the year before, was sweeping California's early two-year-old stakes: the Haggin, the Hollywood Juvenile Championship, the Best Pal Stakes at Del Mar.

Perfect Moon *made* his sire. Malibu Moon hopped onto a Sallee van bound for Kentucky on Friday evening, September 5, 2003. Off-Broadway play goes Broadway. Three weeks later, Brice put Declan's Moon in the gooseneck trailer, drove him thirty miles to Timonium, and bedded him down amid the clatter of sales activity. Declan went to sleep. Next day ... why, even the canted macadam between old fairground barns, center-sloped hard toward storm water drains, couldn't diminish his big swinging walk, his confor-mation, his condition. All perfect. He was the talking horse of the sale, at least the horse we all talked about.

Samantha Siegel arrived from California with Declan on her short list. She loves to shop in Maryland. Always looking for the next Urbane, $25,000-yearling-turned-millionairess. Sam's father, Mace, builds retail malls in California. Buys wholesale horses in Maryland.

Malibu Moon's breeder, B. Wayne Hughes, jetted in on Saturday, before the sale's Monday start.

"Sam is a friend. She said she wouldn't bid against me. But if someone raises my last bid, she'll get in. I told Sam I'm out at 75."

Hughes left the bid with an agent, by noon was flying back to California.

Up from Kentucky came Gabriel Duignan, known as Spider to Irish lads and American mates. An unerring scout of equine tal-ent. Front man for Castleton Lyons Farm, Malibu Moon's new home in the Bluegrass. Spider returned over and over to look at Declan. Brice hung around the shed row like the sideline par-ent of a child star, explaining again and again why he gelded the colt.

"It's the way I raise 'em. Had fillies on his mind. My fillies, the ones right over the fence from him at home. Can't have that. He'll be a better racehorse for it. You'll see."

Muscled up on Brice's home-grown alfalfa, Declan's Moon seemed bigger than other yearlings that filled the oval sales ring. Terence Collier of Fasig-Tipton punched up sale announcements.

"By a red-hot sire. Out of a mare who placed in the Black-Eyed

Susan. And just look at him! You simply can't ask for more in a young horse."

Samantha made the final bid at $125,000. She called her father in California.

"You paid *how much* for a gelding?"

Brice's baby shipped out to Keith Asmussen's ranch in Texas for breaking, arrived at trainer Ron Ellis' barn in California the following spring. Ellis is a detail man. I've seen him sit in the straw of a horse's stall, his legs straddling an ankle, rubbing soothing liniment on tender tendons. A groom's job done by a headline trainer. Happiness lies in the details.

By Christmas, Declan's Moon was the winter-book favorite for the Kentucky Derby. The future was so bright Ellis had to wear shades on covers of the trades, eye-to-eye with a horse he thought capable of greatness. Declan stayed unbeaten, running his record to five-for-five in his first start at three, the Santa Catalina Stakes on March 5. Looking more and more like one for the ages. So fluid, so athletic, so smart.

All systems go for Kentucky.

On Friday, March 11, Ellis felt heat in Declan's left knee. Derby dream just that. The story of one good horse, perhaps a great one, ending in an X-ray.

Before the knee? Final points of call in his races read: 1, 1, 1, 1, 1.

After surgery? 2, 7, 3, 7, 5 ... and so on....

Puzzling reversal of form. He'd work best of twenty. When they'd run, he'd take the lead and stop, or press the pace and stop. The coming of artificial surfaces to California didn't matter. It wasn't his legs. It was his head.

Perhaps it was actually his throat. Seasoned trainers around Clocker's Corner anecdotally observed that racehorses placed under anesthesia sometimes inexplicably do not return to form. Did a tube down a horse's trachea somehow impair the mechanics? Who can say?

Five-for-five before surgery.

One-for-thirteen after.

Cryptic chart notes — dueled, gave way; speed inside, weakened; no response when asked; eased.

By the spring of 2008, the appearance of six-year-old Declan's Moon on the racetrack was like watching an aging boxer buckle after five rounds. Ellis, the most patient of trainers, had nurtured Declan through five campaigns. He wanted a soft landing for the champ, as did the Siegels.

They inquired whether the Kentucky Horse Park would accept Declan into their Hall of Champions. Honestly, even if there had been an open stall, Declan was merely a really good horse, not a great one. He hadn't even earned a million dollars, just $705,647. Too humble for Horse Park stall plaques.

When Kentucky demurred, the Siegels kindly sent Declan back home to Maryland. They knew he'd be appreciated for the glory he'd brought to the locals, for the air of stardom he carries effortlessly. The racing channels announced that Declan's Moon had been retired to stud at Merryland. A friend from Kentucky called.

"Make sure you just sell 'No Guarantee' seasons."

Joe Palmer once wrote a column about the memorable horses pensioned at Greentree Stud. The Gas House Gang, he called them, an alliterative term I've adopted for the gaggle of geldings accumulating at Merryland.

As soon as this show's over, Declan's going out back with the Gas House Gang. And I'll stand on the hill and introduce them one-by-crazy-story-one, like Jack Nicholson did for the colorful cast in One Flew Over the Cuckoo's Nest, as they hijacked the fishing boat.

"Here, racing fans, is the earth-quaking, stakes-shaking, Perfect Moon.

"The next member of the Gas House Gang is the only French steeplechaser named for a Russian czar. Winner of America's Grand National right here in Maryland. The jumping-est old horse you ever saw, Tarsky.

"That obstreperous Appaloosa next to him arrived the year Smarty Jones put slots in Pennsylvania, hence his name, Stinky Jones.

"And the newest moon in our solar system! Maryland-bred Eclipse Award champion! Undefeated two-year-old! One-time favorite for the Kentucky Derby! The one you walked up the hill to see. Give it up for one *really* good horse, homegrown hero Declan's Moon."

Race and (Stakes) Record

YEAR	AGE	STS	1ST	2ND	3RD	EARNED
2004	at 2	4	4 (3)	0 (0)	0 (0)	$507,300
2005	at 3	1	1 (1)	0 (0)	0 (0)	$120,000
2006	at 4	3	0 (0)	1 (0)	1 (1)	$23,000
2007	at 5	7	1 (0)	1 (0)	1 (0)	$53,387
2008	at 6	3	0 (0)	0 (0)	0 (0)	$1,960
Lifetime		**18**	**6 (4)**	**2 (0)**	**2 (1)**	**$705,647**

DESERT AIR

BY AMANDA DUCKWORTH

5

On any given morning at the Thoroughbred Center near Lexington, Kentucky, a dark bay gelding with a small white star can be seen galloping by. His ears are pinned in concentration; his legs, in constant motion.

The horse could be any one of many being put through their paces, but he isn't. Among the horses learning what racing is all about, fourteen-year-old Desert Air, as part of the North American Racing Academy stable, is the one doing the teaching.

However, long before he became a teacher for future jockeys, Desert Air was a top-notch racehorse in his own right for Greg Goodman, who had bought him from his father's estate.

When Goodman and his siblings lost their father, Harold, a prominent Thoroughbred owner and breeder in Texas, in January 1995, they had to figure out how to divvy up his horses. To Greg, one mare and her foal stood out the most, and he decided to buy them from the dispersal of his father's horses.

The mare was Desert Angel, and the foal was her colt, later named Desert Air, who had been born one week before the elder Goodman died.

"There were twenty-five to thirty horses, and those were the only two I bought," said Goodman. "I liked them the most when I was making the decision."

Both Desert Angel and Desert Air more than earned their keep for Goodman, who was born in Houston, Texas, and has been involved with horses most of his life. A year after his father's death, Goodman bought Mt. Brilliant Farm, a historic property near Lexington, Kentucky, that was part of a land grant deeded in 1744. These days he and his wife, Rebecca, who have four children, split their time between the Bluegrass and Lone Star states.

As a broodmare, Desert Angel provided Goodman with his first two horses good enough to run in graded stakes company, and Desert Air did more than run at the top levels — he won. The dark bay went into training with Michael Stidham, who had also trained horses for Harold Goodman, including Desert Air's grade III-winning sire, Manzotti.

"The cool thing about Desert Air is he is a Manzotti, and I had a long history with the family," said Stidham. "He liked what he did, and he liked to train. Every time you sent him over, he tried hard in the races."

In addition to enjoying his job, Desert Air was also built for it. The gelding is well-balanced and has good conformation, which helped keep him sound during a successful seven-year racing career.

On May 17, 1997, at Lone Star Park in Texas, a two-year-old Desert Air made his first start. He ran a decent third that day, a solid second in his next start a month later, and then broke his maiden in his third start on July 16.

After breaking his maiden, Desert Air began running in allowance company and soon thereafter made his stakes debut. He captured the first of seven career stakes victories at the very end of 1998, when he took the Houston Mile Stakes by 6¼ lengths the day after Christmas. His easy win only hinted at the year he would have in 1999.

According to Stidham, a combination of things led to Desert Air's being a successful racehorse. In addition to his excellent conformation, the bay gelding's temperament lent itself to the game. Simply put, Desert Air had a strong will to race.

That desire led Desert Air to six stakes victories in 1999, the most important of which came March 13 at Oaklawn Park in Arkansas when he won the grade III Razorback Handicap over a sloppy track by 1¾ lengths.

"The horse could run on dirt, in the mud; he would sprint, and he would go long," said Goodman. "If you look at his record, it just didn't matter to him. But the Razorback was without a doubt the most exciting because it was my first personal graded win."

Along with the Razorback, Desert Air won the Bob Johnson Memorial, Premiere, Assault, and Jersey Village Stakes as well as the Thanksgiving Handicap as a four-year-old. That year alone he earned $264,300 for his connections, and, appropriately enough, while Desert Air raced at tracks all across the country, he did most of his running in the Southwest.

The handsome bay gelding would go on to race for four more years, but he was never quite as good as he was in 1999. He finished third in the 2000 Diplomat Way Handicap and second in the 2001 Premiere Stakes — the last time he would hit the board in stakes company for Goodman.

In 2002, Desert Air only made one start before minor physical issues took him off the track for a year, giving him a well-deserved break from the races. When he made his eight-year-old debut at Fair Grounds in January 2003, Stidham and Goodman made the decision to enter him in a claiming race. Although any horse running in a claiming race is being offered for sale, Desert Air's connections never thought anyone would actually take their horse.

They were wrong.

"We didn't think we would lose him, but we did," said Stidham.

Dallas Keen claimed Desert Air for $12,500 for owner Michael Franklin. In his first start for his new connections, Desert Air finished third in the 2003 Jersey Village Stakes at Sam Houston Race Park, the only time he hit the board for Keen and Franklin. Stidham claimed him back for $10,000 on May 24, 2003, at Lone

Desert Air winning the 1999 Jersey Village Stakes

Star Park, and, thus, the track where Desert Air made his first start was also where he made his last.

"Greg and I talked about it, and decided, 'Hey, let's claim him back and just retire him so he can live out a good life,' " said Stidham. "He was good to us, for sure. Physically he was still in real good condition. He wasn't going in a bad direction as far as any problems leg-wise go. It is just his age caught up with him a little bit, and he wasn't able to compete at that level anymore."

Desert Air retired with a record of eleven wins, two seconds, and ten thirds in forty-eight career starts. He earned $452,225, with the vast majority of it coming as a de facto homebred for Goodman. Beyond what he gave to Goodman in measurable terms, Desert Air was valuable on another level.

"He means a lot to me and has a lot of sentimental value," said Goodman. "He had a great race career, and it was really fun. I went to all of his races and got to travel around. He was just an awesome horse.

"He was one of those that just kept grounding it out, was always healthy, had a great personality, and was just great to be around. So, after he retired, I wanted to do something with him, but I didn't know what to do."

Desert Air did not just leave an impression on his owner. He also left a lasting mark on those who worked with him on a daily basis for most of his seven-year racing career. He was a kind horse, and Stidham and his staff had fallen in love with him over the years.

Initially, the connections decided to make the gelding Stidham's stable pony, but it soon became evident that wasn't going to work. What made Desert Air such a talented racehorse is also what made finding him a second career tricky. Although the folks in the barn loved him, he never settled down enough to make a good pony. So, the Texas-bred gelding was sent to Mt. Brilliant.

Goodman decided to increase the span of Mt. Brilliant in 2003 by purchasing the adjacent Faraway Farm. That piece of property housed the stallion barn and breeding shed used by Man o' War, and Goodman assumed the responsibility of restoring the historic buildings.

In 2004, Desert Angel, who had produced eight foals including Desert Air and stakes winner Desert Demon, died as the result of colic at age seventeen. It is in the cemetery behind the stallion barn that the Desert Wine mare is buried alongside such horses as Mars and Edith Cavell, stakes winners by Man o' War, and Man o' War's stakes-producing daughters Furlough and Rambler Rose.

"Their mother was very sentimental to me," said Goodman. "I have had some really good mares, but she is the only one I have buried in the cemetery behind Man o' War's barn that has all these great broodmares. She was just special."

Desert Air spent his days grazing at his owner's farm before Goodman came up with another idea for his prized gelding's future. Given Desert Air's physical attributes, Goodman decided he might make a nice eventer and sent him to Chicago to be retrained as a jumper.

"The lady just loved him and worked with him for a couple months. But then she called and said, 'He is a great horse ... but he can't jump. He just won't jump,' explained Goodman. "So she sent him back to us."

After Desert Air's second attempt at a new career fell through, he became a riding horse at Mt. Brilliant. Goodman continued to pay for the upkeep and care of the horse, but wanted to make sure he got exercise as well. Katy Moore, who now works for Darley Australia, rode Desert Air for six to eight months but then began playing polo with Goodman's children, and the gelding was not the right physical type for the sport.

Although Moore still took care of Desert Air, he no longer had an activity that provided mental stimulation. He was doing nothing more than being a pasture pet … until serendipitous timing provided the gelding with the perfect second career.

While Goodman was struggling to find Desert Air a job, Hall of Fame jockey Chris McCarron was starting up the North American Racing Academy, the only school in the country that trains people to be jockeys. In order for students to get hands-on experience, McCarron needed Thoroughbreds that could fill the role of equine teachers.

One day when Goodman was lamenting that Desert Air deserved to have something to do, Gay Fisher, who works at Mt. Brilliant, proposed calling the NARA. They discovered McCarron was looking for more horses for the program, and he came out to inspect the gelding.

At the time, Desert Air was sporting a long winter coat, had put on a few pounds, and was muddy from being out in the paddock. Upon seeing him, McCarron was not sure the gelding would work for the program, but confident that he would be a good fit, everyone at Mt. Brilliant requested some time to clean him up and trim him down.

McCarron agreed to that request and returned a few months later to find Desert Air looking like a million dollars. And so, for the fourth time since being retired, Desert Air was about to embark on another career.

Although he was in good physical shape for his new job, the gelding's mental sharpness was still a concern. If Desert Air was too determined to race, as he had been bred and trained to do, he would not make a suitable riding horse for the school.

"I am usually the first person to get on any new horses we acquire, and I put them through their paces to make sure they aren't blind, crippled, or crazy before we accept them into the program," McCarron said. "The first few days, I just rode (Desert Air) around the stable area at the training center. You could tell he was having some flashbacks."

Being put through his paces during those first few days, Desert Air was again in danger of being sent home. With his tail up over his back, the gelding would prance on his toes and snort out his approval of being back at the track. But after he was given a chance to settle down, Desert Air quickly got into the routine.

Desert Air, who answers to "Desi" these days, became part of the NARA program in 2006, the first year it was up and running. Desi required very little retraining as he is used to teach future jockeys how to handle, gallop, breeze, and ride racehorses.

"He was a real generous horse on the track, and he has been very generous with us as well," said McCarron. "It took him no time at all to adjust. Desi is without question the most talented horse we have in the barn."

Because Desi has not forgotten his racing days, he isn't the first horse new students will get on. Rather, he is ridden when they are more advanced.

"They have to keep their wits about them when they are around him," said McCarron. "He doesn't have a mean bone in his body, other than he's a typical strong and aggressive Thoroughbred when he wants to be. He is very kind. When he is on the track, he is all business and very professional.

"However, he pulls like a freight train. He's not only served to give the students a good ride every morning, he's gotten them very fit. He makes them work hard when they are on his back."

Desi's routine at the NARA fluctuates, depending on the level of experience the riders have at a given time. He has been known to gallop four times a week, have a workout once a week, and be turned out on the weekend. At other times, because he is still so strong, he is not breezed in an effort to calm him down for new students.

While some of the horses in the program are not the most gifted at racing, Desert Air is. As a result, when NARA's inaugural class put on a graduation race prior to the High Hope Steeplechase at the Kentucky Horse Park in May 2008, he went off as one of the favorites.

The six-furlong turf race, called the "Catch a Riding Star," was a non-sanctioned event, meaning it did not count toward any of the official records of the horses, but it did simulate what a real race would be like. However, racing luck is always important, and the best horse on paper does not always win.

In the graduation race, Desert Air's rider kept him extremely wide and gave him too much to do. The gelding finished fifth and probably ran closer to seven furlongs than the six he was meant to, but that did little to diminish his importance to the program.

Desert Air now teaches riding skills to aspiring jockeys.

Desert Air not only helps those currently attending the school, but is also there for those who may need a refresher course. One member of NARA's initial graduating class, Brad Wilson, was back in Kentucky in the fall of 2008 exercising the program's horses in order to regain his riding fitness after an injury, and Desi certainly helped with that goal.

Wilson admits that while the gelding has mellowed a bit since joining the program, he is still a challenging ride.

"He's still really strong, but he's just doing his job," said Wilson. "I have loved him ever since I started getting on him."

And so while there was a bit of trial and error involved, Desert Air finally found the perfect second career. It comes as no surprise that he excels at it, since it is allowing him to do what he always did best.

"I am glad he is getting to do this and is well taken care of," said Goodman. "This horse loved everything about the racetrack. You know how some people say they never spend a bad day fishing? I think that horse never spent a bad day at the racetrack. He loved it and thrived on it, so it is great he gets to live out his life at least simulating racing. I am really happy for him and really appreciate what Chris has done."

McCarron echoed those sentiments, saying: "We feel very fortunate to be able to put a horse back into doing something. I firmly believe that most Thoroughbreds really like engaging with people, they like training, and they like running. Desi is a gem. He's

At the Thoroughbred Center, Desert Air thrives on routine.

a teacher now, and the students learn more from the horses than they do from me."

Throughout his life, Desert Air has done his best to please the people around him, and when the time comes that he is finally ready truly to retire, there is little doubt that everyone who has been involved with him will make sure he is well taken care of.

Until then, anyone watching the horses work at the Thoroughbred Center may see a dark bay gelding with a white star and think he is getting a lesson, when in reality, he is the one doing the teaching.

Race and (Stakes) Record

YEAR	AGE	STS	1ST	2ND	3RD	EARNED
1997	at 2	7	1 (0)	1 (0)	4 (0)	$26,905
1998	at 3	13	3 (1)	0 (0)	3 (2)	$82,865
1999	at 4	9	6 (6)	0 (0)	0 (0)	$264,300
2000	at 5	7	1 (0)	0 (0)	1 (1)	$54,985
2001	at 6	5	0 (0)	1 (1)	1 (0)	$18,300
2002	at 7	1	0 (0)	0 (0)	0 (0)	$1,020
2003	at 8	6	0 (0)	0 (0)	1 (1)	$3,850
Lifetime		**48**	**11 (7)**	**2 (1)**	**10 (4)**	**$452,225**

FIGHTING FURRARI

By TRACY GANTZ

6

Plain, small, and slow — Fighting Furrari didn't have characteristics that ensured his success as a racehorse. They did, however, turn him into a movie star.

Fighting Furrari became one of ten horses who played Seabiscuit in the 2003 Academy Award-nominated movie. He continues the role today at Santa Anita Park, greeting fans who take tram tours of the historic Southern California racetrack and attend the races. In his down time, he competes on the local hunter-jumper circuit under the name Seabiscuit, earning ribbons and posing for photos with kids who ride his competitors.

"When he goes to a show, the little girls just line up to have their pictures taken with him," said Candace Coder-Chew, director of print and graphics at Santa Anita.

Coder-Chew manages Fighting Furrari's care, both at Santa Anita and at the Encanto Equestrian Center in Duarte, California. Known as "Fred" at the barn, the small bay gelding manages to snag more than his fair share of carrots at the expense of his much-larger paddock mate, usually a pony from the racetrack on R&R.

"Everybody knows Fred — he's got his own fan club," said Janie Steiner. The resident hunter-jumper trainer at Encanto, Steiner oversees Fred's show horse training.

Fighting Furrari began life as many racehorses do, born in Kentucky. Bred by Richard Shepard, he was foaled April 11, 1998, to the broodmare Fit for Fun. His sire, Momsfurrari, won nearly $500,000 on Midwestern and Florida racetracks, but Fred's racing career would sputter and stall for Shepard on smaller tracks in northern Kentucky and Ohio

By the time Dutch and Linda Hatcher, who owned and trained racehorses in Lexington, Kentucky, encountered Fighting Furrari at River Downs outside of Cincinnati in July 2002, he had managed to win only one race amid a flurry of decisively mediocre performances.

"He was just as fat as a little pig," Linda Hatcher recalled. "He was so round you could roll a watermelon on his back."

When Fred failed to win yet again, Dutch Hatcher, who Linda says "likes to horse trade," made the owner a cash offer that was quickly accepted. Dutch and Linda felt that Fighting Furrari wasn't as fit as he could be, and they thought they might be able to improve his performances at the track.

"We took him back to where we were training horses at the Kentucky Training Center," Linda said. "He cleaned up every bit of hay and grain that we gave him."

Linda began exercising Fred in an effort to get him fit. "He went like a saddle horse," she said. "We worked with him and proceeded to teach him to go forward and things like that. I think we ran him two or three times, and he showed a little improvement."

Fred's improvement failed to earn him very much money, however. In what would become his final start, he finished sixth at Turfway Park in northern Kentucky on September 29, 2002, for a $58 paycheck. Then good luck arrived in the form of Jerry Wilson, a horse broker from West Virginia.

Wilson was canvassing Kentucky, looking for horses that could be used in racing scenes for *Seabiscuit*. The movie was being filmed at Keeneland in Lexington, Kentucky, and would later move to Santa Anita, the track where Seabiscuit made most of his starts during the 1930s.

"He told us he was looking for horses for the movie," Linda Hatcher said. "When we brought out Fighting Furrari, the guy immediately said, 'I've got a spot for him.' "

Not only did the movie require a string of racehorses for the re-creation of races, director Gary Ross and head wrangler Rusty Hendrickson needed several horses to play Seabiscuit, a small, plain bay colt with no white markings. Wilson saw that Fred was a dead ringer for Seabiscuit, which is why he snapped up the gelding as soon as he saw him.

Hendrickson can sum up a horse's movie potential quickly. A Montana rancher, he is one of the most respected horse wranglers in the movie business. His credits include *Dances With Wolves*, *The Horse Whisperer*, *Wyatt Earp*, and, following the release of *Seabiscuit*, the well-received films *Dreamer*, *Flicka*, and *3:10 to Yuma*.

"A movie horse is very different from a racehorse," Hendrickson said. "You actually need a very quiet, calm horse to be on camera."

Usually, Thoroughbreds don't do well in films, according to

Hendrickson, who has had more luck with Quarter Horses. In fact, one of the Seabiscuits was a Quarter Horse that Hendrickson still owns.

"Thoroughbreds aren't for everyday movie stuff, but this one was as good a one as you'll find," Hendrickson said of Fred.

Hendrickson noted that Fred had some breathing problems, which must have compromised his racing ability. For that reason, the wrangler didn't use him in many racing shots. Instead, Fred excelled in close-ups and winner's circle scenes. He and Hendricks' Quarter Horse were the two most often ridden by *Seabiscuit* star Tobey Maguire, who played jockey Red Pollard.

"We rode Fighting Furrari a lot," Hendrickson recalled. "He wasn't a deadhead — he had life. He acted like a racehorse at first, but it didn't take a lot to get him quiet."

Two of Fred's biggest scenes occur during Seabiscuit's match race with War Admiral. Hall of Fame jockey Gary Stevens, who played jockey George Woolf, is aboard Fred when Seabiscuit returns triumphantly to the winner's circle after defeating War Admiral.

With Randy Newman's score soaring on the soundtrack, Stevens rides Fred to the screams of extras, pumping his fist into the air.

"That was the most fun scene," Stevens said.

Fred arched his neck and trotted confidently amid all the noise, strutting like the champion racehorse he wasn't.

Hendrickson also used Fred in the match race winner's circle. Wearing a blanket of flowers and carrying Stevens, Fred walked into the winner's circle and stood quietly, even when things went wrong. "We used those cameras with those old-fashioned flashbulbs," Hendrickson said. "One of the extras came up into the horse's face and the bulb hit the horse in the face. It didn't faze him at all."

Stevens also recalls the moment.

"The flashbulb actually exploded," the jockey said. "There was glass everywhere, and he just stood there. It scared me more than it scared him. There were probably thirty people in the winner's circle. It's a good thing it wasn't one of the other horses."

Six years later, in mid-2008, Fred showed similar serenity when filming an episode of the television series *The Cleaner*. In the climactic scene, the jockey is celebrating in the winner's circle when he dies and falls off the horse. The stuntman didn't need many takes to get the job done.

"Fred stood like a statue," said Coder-Chew, who with her husband, Thoroughbred trainer Matt Chew, often supplies horses such as Fred to film crews.

Fred didn't take to every scene in *Seabiscuit*, though.

"We had him at the train with confetti and stuff," Hendrickson said. "He didn't want any part of that, so we had to use another horse."

Fred also failed in one of his racing scenes, the stretch run against War Admiral. Hall of Fame jockey Chris McCarron was a consultant on the film, designing the racing sequences, and he played War Admiral's jockey, Charley Kurtsinger. He recalled that Fred actually lost the famous match race.

"I was riding Cobra Fight, who was a 17.1-hand gangly horse who just kind of galloped along," said McCarron. "Gary was on Fighting Furrari on the inside. When they yelled 'action' and Gary says, 'So long, Charley,' we got to riding. Cobra Flight just took off."

Fred's quiet temperament made him a good movie horse.

McCarron and Stevens didn't want *Seabiscuit* to look like other racing movies, where the jockeys are obviously holding back their horses to let the correct one win. After Fred lost the race to Cobra Flight, one of the other Seabiscuits, Rich in Dallas, replaced Fred for the actual race footage and won by several lengths as required in the script.

Once the movie finished filming, the crew found homes for all of the horses. Producers Frank Marshall and Kathleen Kennedy thought Fred would be perfect for Skyline Guest Ranch, a dude ranch in Telluride, Colorado, that bordered property they owned. Hendrickson delivered the horse there himself in 2003.

For a while, Fred worked at the ranch, going out on rides and acting as the local celebrity. It didn't take long, though, for him to return to California. Santa Anita management was interested in Fred as the cornerstone of its tram tour, a free weekend morning outing that upon success of the movie was repackaged into the Seabiscuit Tram Tour.

McCarron, Santa Anita's general manager at the time, was instrumental in bringing Fred back to the track. Once Fred arrived, fresh and wanting some exercise, McCarron rode him around the Santa Anita barn area, once with embarrassing results.

"It had rained and the backstretch was very muddy," McCarron said. "Fighting Furrari got to playing. He threw his head between his knees, and when he went up, I came off."

McCarron, covered in mud, had to call Coder-Chew and confess to losing the horse.

"Here I was, the general manager of Santa Anita, he drops me, and I'm chasing him around the barn area," said McCarron, who several years later gleefully tells the story on himself. Fred skedaddled to a quiet corner of the barn area, where McCarron eventually caught him.

Santa Anita constructed an outdoor pen for Fred near the west entrance to the grandstand. Fred began greeting not only tram tours there, but anyone who attended the races and wanted to stop by. He also visits the infield during several Infield Family Fun days scheduled throughout the racing season. A handler dons Seabiscuit silks, telling people about the movie, while Fred poses for more photos.

"I've taught him a couple of tricks, to nod his head yes when asked if he wants a carrot and how to bow," Coder-Chew said. "Sometimes, I don't have a carrot, and he'll keep doing the trick

At Santa Anita Park, Fred greets fans in his role as Seabiscuit.

to get the treat. I've had ask the crowd on a few occasions for peppermints, an Altoid, or a Tic Tac."

Fred accepts all contributions as his rightful due, completely immersed in his role as the mighty Seabiscuit.

"One man, Mike, is his biggest fan," Coder-Chew said. "He adores this horse. He comes to see him every single weekend and brings him an entire bag of carrots. If I'm doing a tram tour and Fred hears Mike, he won't pay any more attention to me. Fred has a pretty big group of groupies."

Several Santa Anita employees also visit Fred regularly, arriving with carrots, peppermints, and other enticements.

Racing occurs at Santa Anita for about half the year — several months in the winter and spring and a few more weeks in the fall. That left Fred with time for a new career. In 2007 he became a show horse and in the process gave teenager Randi Pomrehn an emotional lift she needed after weathering a double tragedy.

While Fred was starring in the movie and working at the dude ranch, Randi was developing into one of trainer Kellie Cerin's most promising riding students. Cerin, the wife of Thoroughbred racehorse trainer Vladimir Cerin, successfully turned racehorses into show horses, and Randi at only thirteen had already graduated from hunters to jumpers.

But in early 2007 on a vacation to Mexico with her husband, Kellie died suddenly of a heart attack at age fifty-one. Randi was devastated to lose her beloved trainer, and only three months later, Randi's horse, Tiki, died following colic surgery.

Kellie's students had often competed at shows that Steiner conducted. Following Kellie's death, Janie welcomed Kellie's young

Fred is on the muscle as he parades near the grandstand.

students to her barn, Randi included. Randi and Tiki were doing well under Janie's tutelage, qualifying for a hunter medal show that fall, when several bouts with colic ultimately killed the horse.

"I was distraught — we were all crying," Janie said. "I thought, 'We have got to find Randi another horse.' One day Candie and I were having a chit-chat, when she said, 'Why don't you get on Fred and try him out?' I popped him over a few cross-rails — he'd never jumped before — and I liked him."

Janie and Candie came up with a plan to let Randi ride Fred until she was able to get a new horse.

"I thought that he would be a project that Randi could sink her teeth into," Janie said. "I told her that I had a horse that needed to be ridden. She had been crying for Tiki, and after she rode Fred the first time, she came off him with a smile. He blossomed, she blossomed — they blossomed together."

Randi liked Fred right away, even though she soon saw through his self-satisfaction.

"He didn't know anything, but he acted like he knew everything," Randi said. "He learned very quickly. If he does something wrong and you correct him, he quickly does it right."

Randi rode Fred through the summer of 2007. Just before school began in the fall, she tried him in a nighttime show.

"He did okay, but we didn't get any ribbons," she said. "He'd never been to a show before."

Randi's trainer felt differently because she knew what an accomplishment it was for both horse and rider. "At that first show he was awesome," Janie said. "Anything new, he just picks it up so quickly."

During the off season, Fred enjoys jumping with rider Randi Pomrehn.

When Fred and Randi competed in three classes at the 2007 Victory Horse Show in early September, they came away with a first and second in two schooling jumper classes.

"He was a star," said Randi proudly.

Steiner eventually found another ex-racehorse, now named Tucker, for Randi. A bowed tendon had ended Tucker's racing career, and it would be several months before Randi would be able to even ride him, let alone show him. In the meantime, she could continue to ride Fred.

"He's genuine," Janie said. "He's also very agile. Jumpers need to go clean and quick, and that's where Fred does well."

Fred's two jobs dovetailed with each other. He could spend the fall and winter entertaining racetrack crowds at Santa Anita and

Randi and Fred earn a blue ribbon in the show ring.

return to the horse show circuit in the summer, when Randi was out of school. They built upon their initial success in 2007 the following year.

At a show in May 2008, ten-year-old Fred, under show name Seabiscuit, and fifteen-year-old Randi competed in six classes. They won pre-training jumpers and low children's/adult amateur jumpers and finished second in training jumpers. In July they won a pre-training jumper class to qualify for a large year-end show that fall.

"He's up to jumping 3 feet to 3-foot-3 now," said Randi.

Fred's dual jobs would keep most horses busy. But he continued to take on more. He frequently visits Sacramento, California's capital, to meet and greet state legislators, and he hasn't given up his movie career. In mid-2008, Fred was one of the horses used at

Santa Anita to film part of the Johnny Depp/Christian Bale 1930s gangster movie *Public Enemies*, directed by Michael Mann of *Miami Vice* fame.

"Michael Mann had a hand-held camera taking close-up shots of the horse," Coder-Chew recalled. "He was in Fred's face, and Fred didn't flinch. He's been so good for anything we've asked of him."

Coder-Chew has taken Fred to Sacramento several times. Fred, tacked up in racing gear and with Candie or another rider wearing the Seabiscuit silks, stands right out on the lawn in front of the Capitol building. California assembly members and senators line up to get their pictures taken with him as eagerly as the kids at the horse shows.

"He travels very well," Coder-Chew said. "He's really sensible about things. I try to limit his appearances to three or four hours. Otherwise, he can get cranky. But often so many people want their pictures taken that we're there for five or six hours."

Fred played Seabiscuit for the entire eighteen-day run of the California State Fair in August 2008. He first participated in the Friends of the Fair Gala a week before the fair began.

"We had him in a 12' x 12' pen in the middle of the room where the silent auction took place," Coder-Chew said. "He didn't get the least bit excited. He let people pet him, and he was the star attraction."

During the fair, Fred led the post parade at the races on opening day and for major stakes. He participated in the opening ceremonies of the fair's rodeo and was the main attraction in the fair's Cavalcade of Horses exhibit, though Shadowfax from the Lord of the Rings movies also drew plenty of attention.

Fred returned to Santa Anita in time for the 2008 fall Oak Tree Racing Association meeting, which featured the rich Breeders' Cup races. He will likely continue to play Seabiscuit at Santa Anita and throughout California for many years to come.

"He always seems happy to go on a new adventure," said Coder-Chew.

				Race and (Stakes) Record			
YEAR	**AGE**	**STS**	**1ST**	**2ND**	**3RD**		**EARNED**
2001	at 3	2	0 (0)	0 (0)	0 (0)		$85
2002	at 4	14	1 (0)	0 (0)	1 (0)		$4,850
Lifetime		**16**	**1 (0)**	**(0)**	**1 (0)**		**$4,935**

FUNNY CIDE

By Claire Novak

Funny Cide came to the Kentucky Horse Park on a crisp autumn day in 2008, as a chill wind blew in from the north and falling leaves drifted down to the pastures. The leaves matched the color of the chestnut gelding's wooly coat and the wind bolstered his spirits. Racing fans and reporters who had followed his career through thirty-eight starts remarked that they had hardly seen him so happy, so animated, since his Triple Crown campaign in 2003.

In a paddock near the park's Hall of Champions, legendary miler Da Hoss eyed photographers and moved closer to the octagonal viewing stand, part of a notable welcoming committee that included the great Cigar, who cast a regal eye upon a nearby camera crew. In moments, the newest member of the hall would take his place with Da Hoss and Cigar alongside fellow residents Alysheba, Kona Gold, CH Gypsy Supreme, Western Dreamer, and Staying Together.

Funny Cide's fans had driven from Cincinnati, flown in from New York, even traveled from Arkansas and places between to watch their eight-year-old hero retire from the rigors of the racetrack for good. They huddled in winter coats, clutching hot cups of "Funny Cider," watching the Kentucky Derby and Preakness winner ham it up just for them.

Funny Cide was in his element. He circled the viewing ring in the hands of barn manager Cathy Roby, ears flicking, taking in the scene. One week earlier he'd shipped down from the New York barn of trainer Barclay Tagg, where he'd served as a stable pony since his retirement from racing in 2007. He spent a week at WinStar Farm, the breeding operation in Versailles, Kentucky that stands his sire, Distorted Humor. He handled the transition like a pro. Now he was taking in his new home.

It had been five years since Funny Cide wowed the nation on a Triple Crown chase that began with a pipe dream, ended beyond his owner's wildest expectations. He brought hope to small-time

Funny Cide gets a warm welcome at the Kentucky Horse Park.

operations, inspired thousands of fans, appeared on his own Web site, and had an extensive line of products bearing his name.

Bred in New York by WinStar in cooperation with McMahon Thoroughbreds, Funny Cide sold as a yearling for $22,000 and was later purchased privately for $75,000 as a two-year-old by Sackatoga Stable, a group of small-town friends. He started under the syndicate's colors at fourteen different tracks, bringing home $3,529,412 and becoming the highest-earning New York-bred in racing history. He also earned an Eclipse Award for champion three-year-old colt and scored nine stakes wins — including the grade one Jockey Club Gold Cup — in a racing career that spanned six seasons.

Until Funny Cide, a gelding had not won the Derby since Clyde Van Dusen took the 1929 edition. The latter became a stable pony in California, so it seemed only fitting his modern predecessor should follow in his hoofprints. A poster child for healthy Thoroughbred retirement, Funny Cide turned heads on the backside of every racetrack he visited. He became the subject of more media coverage than almost any other retired runner, inspiring *The Courier-Journal* reporter Gregory Hall to call him "the most famous stable pony at any racetrack in the country," while Brendan O'Meara of *The Saratogian* described him as "your Wal-Mart greeter, with more muscle."

It was an ideal life, but a nagging back injury left the gelding unhappy under saddle. Tagg and Jack Knowlton, managing partner of Sackatoga Stable, knew it was time for a change.

Funny Cide's renown made him an ideal candidate for the Kentucky Horse Park's Hall of Champions, and thus the gelding was greeted in a manner befitting his stature. He relished the limelight,

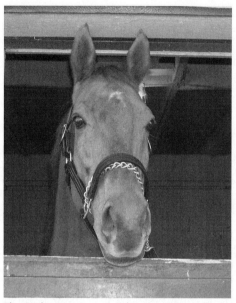

The Derby winner surveys his new surroundings.

posing for the cameras with the bearing of a superstar, ears pricked, neck arched.

"He really is the people's horse because of what he accomplished on the racetrack and because he stuck around for so many years," Knowlton told the attentive fans who had gathered to celebrate Funny Cide's arrival at the Horse Park. "And then he gave the industry hope; he showed the small players that anyone can do this and win. This is the premiere place for a racehorse like him to be retired, and this way so many of his fans will be able to see him, and new fans will be able to meet him."

Now, in a spacious stall once occupied by Bold Forbes and Quar-

Funny Cide's Race and (Stakes) Record

YEAR	AGE	STS	1ST	2ND	3RD	EARNED
2002	at 2	3	3 (2)	0 (0)	0 (0)	$136,185
2003	at 3	8	2 (2)	2 (2)	2 (2)	$1,963,200
2004	at 4	10	3 (2)	2 (2)	3 (3)	$1,075,100
2005	at 5	3	0 (0)	0 (0)	0 (0)	$45,834
2006	at 6	10	2 (2)	2 (1)	1 (1)	$235,284
2007	at 7	4	1 (1)	0 (0)	2 (2)	$73,809
Lifetime		**38**	**11 (9)**	**6 (5)**	**8 (4)**	**$3,529,412**

ter Horse champion Sgt. Pepper Feature, the gutsy gelding is living out a life of ease — the leader of a select group of horses that once competed at the highest levels of racing and now have new and varied jobs.

Two years after Funny Cide won the Preakness, another hard-knocking performer stepped into the starting gate at Pimlico Race Course. Scrappy T was a big brown monster of a colt with an unpredictable personality — one of his first handlers chose to slide the feed bowl under the stall door rather than face his aggression. But that fighting spirit served him well on the track, and he rolled into the second leg of the Triple Crown off a solid score in the Withers Stakes at Aqueduct. He had never been worse than third and had two other wins to his name, including a score in Aqueduct's Count Fleet Handicap.

The Kentucky-bred son of Fit to Fight raced well within striking distance for the early portion of the 2005 Preakness and had the lead under jockey Ramon Dominguez turning for home. It appeared as if his only threat would come from Afleet Alex, the third-place finisher in that year's Kentucky Derby. But when Dominguez set his mount down for the drive with a powerful left-handed stroke of the whip, the temperamental colt recoiled and thrust himself directly into the path of the oncoming Afleet Alex, who was closing on the outside under jockey Jeremy Rose. Afleet Alex clipped heels and went to his knees but amazingly rebounded to win by 4¾ lengths. Scrappy T finished second. He would never win another race.

Trainer Robbie Bailes sent "Scrappy" to the starting gate seven more times, including a runner-up finish in the 2005 Indiana Derby (grade II) and four comeback starts in 2008 after two years away from the track. The colt had been gelded, and his edgy attitude disappeared. But he failed to return to his winning ways, so after a fourth-place finish at Delaware Park in July 2008, owner Marshall Dowell called it quits. Scrappy T retired with a 3-7-2 record from seventeen starts and earnings of $645,919.

Today, the seven-year-old gelding has a new job — that of a foxhunter in Powhatan, Virginia — as a mount for horsewoman Danielle Mason. His milder manners have him snuffing up peppermints and posing for photos for the local newspaper. He's come a long way since his racing days, and he's finally home.

Another Triple Crown contender fortunate enough to live out his days in happy retirement is Cavonnier. The gutsy gelding — whose runner-up finish to Grindstone in the 1996 Kentucky Derby thrilled thousands — is still robust and reveling in his retirement at owner Barbara Walter's Vine Hill Ranch near Sebastopol, California. Scampering up and down the lush green hills, he plays pasture mate to the dozen or so yearlings still bred by Walter following the 2003 death of her husband, Robert Walter. And every season, on Cavonnier Stakes Day, the horse makes a guest appearance at the nearby Sonoma County Fair.

The now sixteen-year-old son of Battonier broke his maiden at

Scrappy T's Race and (Stakes) Record

YEAR	AGE	STS	1ST	2ND	3RD	EARNED
2004	at 2	5	1 (0)	4 (0)	0 (0)	$55,800
2005	at 3	8	2 (2)	3 (3)	2 (2)	$584,197
2008	at 6	4	0 (0)	0 (0)	0 (0)	$5,922
Lifetime		**17**	**3 (2)**	**7 (3)**	**2 (2)**	**$645,919**

that same location, eventually showing such talent that Walter sent him to Southern California to be campaigned by Bob Baffert along the Triple Crown trail. In his three-year-old season, Cavonnier amassed quite a following with his wins in the Santa Anita Derby and El Camino Real Derby. Having come within a whisker of winning the Kentucky Derby in a photo finish that took the judges approximately five minutes to decide, he ran fourth in the Preakness and later suffered a bowed tendon in his right foreleg during the Belmont Stakes.

The quick thinking of jockey Chris McCarron likely saved the 1996 California Horse of the Year from further injury as he pulled out of the competition. Cavonnier was sent to the University of California, Davis, for treatment. There, an experimental drug called Bapten (which was reported to promote the healing of torn tendon fibers by modifying the formation of scar tissue) was used to help heal the injury. Although Bapten was later discontinued due to a lack of interest, it enabled Cavonnier to return to training over the uphill gallop at Vine Hill. He went on to win the Ack Ack Stakes at Santa Anita before retiring for good in 1999 with earnings of more than $1.2 million.

Now, on Cavonnier Day, the dark bay gelding ships to the racetrack at the Sonoma County Fair for his annual parade before the crowd. Of course, everyone cheers and hollers and claps and hoots and whistles, and the old showman eats it up. He arches his neck, pricks his ears, lifts his tail high. He remembers these grandstands and this winner's circle. He turns his head to stare at the crowd as if to say, "Keep going, clap for me, I know what this track is for!"

Barbara Walter still thrills in the memories of Cavonnier's campaign, crediting her late husband's commitment to animal husbandry as the reason for the gelding's retirement to their farm. While Robert Walter bred horses to compete at the highest levels of the game, he was also a man of integrity who felt responsible for every horse he ever ran.

"Cavonnier did have a couple races after recovering from his tendon injury, and then Mr. W decided that if he wasn't going to come back at the same level, then we weren't going to force it," Barbara Walter said. "It all comes down to one thing — love of the horse. Now Cavonnier is in a pasture just at the gate to my house; he knows my car and I always roll the window down and stop, and if he's near the fence, he comes over for his treat of carrots. He'll always be king of the roost."

Unfortunately, not all classic contenders have been treated with that concept of reciprocity. In Louisville, another Kentucky Derby runner is living out a much-deserved life of ease — but unlike Funny Cide and Cavonnier, his story got worse before it got better.

Phantom On Tour, the official "spokeshorse" of the Kentucky Derby Museum, finished second or third in eight starts leading up to the 1997 edition of the Run for the Roses. After running sixth in

Cavonnier's Race and (Stakes) Record

YEAR	AGE	STS	1ST	2ND	3RD	EARNED
1995	at 2	9	4 (3)	2 (1)	1 (1)	$190,158
1996	at 3	7	2 (2)	1 (1)	1 (1)	$949,240
1998	at 5	1	1 (1)	0 (0)	0 (0)	$52,935
1999	at 6	3	3 (0)	0 (0)	0 (0)	$9,332
2000	at 7	2	1 (0)	0 (0)	0 (0)	$52,500
Lifetime		**23**	**8 (6)**	**3 (2)**	**2 (2)**	**$1,254,165**

Phantom on Tour's Race and (Stakes) Record

YEAR	AGE	STS	1ST	2ND	3RD	EARNED
1996	at 2	4	3 (2)	1 (0)	0 (0)	$76,605
1997	at 3	5	2 (2)	2 (2)	0 (0)	$219,000
1998	at 4	8	2 (2)	2 (1)	1 (1)	$421,810
2001	at 7	3	0 ()	1 (0)	0 ()	$7,190
Lifetime		**20**	**7 (6)**	**6 (3)**	**1 (1)**	**$724,605**

the Derby for trainer Lynn Whiting, he rebounded to enjoy a successful four-year-old season with victories in Oaklawn's Crabapple Stakes and the New Orleans Handicap. But when retired to stud at the end of 1998, the son of Tour d'Or proved infertile. Horseman Noel Hickey, who had purchased Phantom On Tour as a stallion prospect, passed the distinctive chestnut on to a Connecticut woman who said she would retrain him to be a riding horse. He thought his runner was going to a good home.

Instead, thirty-three months later, Phantom On Tour resurfaced in a claiming race at Philadelphia Park. His struggles to compete against horses far below his former level had concerned fans — including Hickey — scrambling to save him from the possibility of a catastrophic breakdown or a trip to the slaughterhouse. As is often the case with horse rescue, a grassroots effort was launched to guarantee the deserving runner a permanent retirement and the safety of a loving home. When officials at Churchill Downs and its sister track, Calder Race Course, heard of the former Derby contender's plight, they immediately contributed funds to get him off the track for good.

And so, with help from the Thoroughbred Retirement Foundation (TRF), Phantom On Tour became the Kentucky Derby Museum's mascot, taking up residence in a paddock behind the museum, where he provides fans with a visual example of the benefits of Thoroughbred adoption. But the Derby Museum isn't Phantom's only home. He also spends time at the Thoroughbred Retirement Foundation's Blackburn Correctional Complex in Lexington, where inmates and racehorses find a path to recovery — from life on the streets, from life on the track — together.

At Blackburn, convicts groom and train horses such as the former Kentucky Derby contender, runners whose banged up knees and swollen fetlocks prevent them from pursuing future victories. The Thoroughbreds, many of them available for adoption, receive dedicated care as part of the prison's job-training program. The inmates receive a sense of purpose and responsibility from their assignments. The TRF has taken full advantage of prison programs, which are in high demand among the convicts whose names appear on lengthy waiting lists each season. These programs allow the organization to expand while obtaining voluntary labor and land from locations such as the Wallkill Correctional Facility in New York and the Charles H. Hickey School for youthful offenders in Maryland.

Former stakes contender Little Cliff shares a story similar to Phantom On Tour's, of coming within a whiskered nostril of the slaughterhouse and prompting a call for vigilant supervision by Thoroughbred owners. By Gulch, the Nick Zito trainee ran twenty-seven times to earn a 3-3-5 record and $202,762 in purses, initially campaigning in grade I races such as the Blue Grass Stakes and the Haskell Invitational.

Little Cliff failed to demonstrate the needed stamina to maintain a place in Robert LaPenta's top-drawer operation, so he eventually descended through the claiming ranks to become a part of Robert Levin and Sheila Austrach's LA Buzz Stable. There, his career took a grim turn. Injured in a $10,000 claiming race at Philadelphia Park on March 1, 2008, he finished seventh of nine and earned $170 for trainer Ramon Preciado. Shortly thereafter, rescue activist Christy Sheidy, co-founder of the group Another Chance 4 Horses, discovered the five-year-old gelding in a direct-to-kill pen in New Holland, Pennsylvania. He had become one of the approximately 7,000 Thoroughbreds whose careers end at the slaughterhouse each year.

News of Little Cliff's situation spread like wildfire through the industry, with major publications picking up the story of his rescue. Zito and LaPenta both contributed significant funds to bring him back to a safe home, and the bay runner was turned out to recover from the traumatic ordeal. Even without returning to work under saddle, he raised major awareness of the need for responsible Thoroughbred ownership.

Other top performers such as millionaire sprinter Shake You Down and champion steeplechasers Correggio and McDynamo are also doing their parts for that cause while living out their later days in happy retirement.

Shake You Down, a Florida-bred gelding by Montbrook, won twenty-two of his sixty-five lifetime starts including six stakes races, among them the True North Breeders' Cup Handicap. The winner of three straight graded stakes at Calder in 2003, he earned more than $1.4 million for trainer Scott Lake and owner Robert Cole

Jr. before retiring safe and sound in 2007 to a permanent home at TRF's Florida division at the Marion County Correctional Institution. In 2008 he was honored during Calder's Festival of the Sun Retired Thoroughbred Ceremony.

Correggio is also a TRF resident, stabled at the foundation's Montpelier estate in Orange, Virginia. The 1996 champion steeplechaser was donated to TRF in 2003 by his owner, Bill Lickle, who hoped to use his runner's fame to help promote the organization and its cause. An Irish-bred son of Sadler's Wells, Correggio won all four starts during his 1996 season, including the Breeders' Cup Grand National and the Colonial Cup. He retired in 1998 with earnings of $274,657 and a 6-3-2 record from fifteen starts.

McDynamo, a three-time Eclipse Award winner as champion steeplechaser (2003, 2005, 2006), rocketed to the top of the sport with major victories that included seven consecutive races at Far Hills — among them consecutive runnings of the Grand National — before retiring as the sport's earnings leader with more than $1.3 million in purses. The Dynaformer gelding retired to life as a foxhunter at owner Michael Moran's Pennsylvania farm, taking to the fields and fences with the same gusto he demonstrated under racing saddle.

And so, with their greatest achievements behind them, some of the industry's most talented runners still enrich the sport. Most importantly, they reflect the unlimited potential of the breed, providing fans and members of the racing industry alike with a tangible example of Thoroughbred retirement as it should be. They are champions still.

GETAWAY HALL

By Jennifer Bryant

8

The Standardbred pacer Getaway Hall made local headlines in June 2008 when he was found grazing along Delaware Route 71 near Middletown, a lead rope dangling from his halter.

Had the thirteen-year-old gelding been abandoned? newspapers speculated. Was this yet another grim economic case study or a sad commentary on the plight of the retired racehorse?

Probably not, say those who know the horse. But Getaway Hall's story contains a couple of surprise twists nonetheless — and it is a cautionary tale of sorts.

Getaway Hall (Cambest—Justascape, by Landslide) had genteel beginnings. Bred by the venerable Walnut Hall Stock Farm in verdant Lexington, Kentucky, he was born April 26, 1995. The farm itself is part of a 9,000-acre tract given as a land grant by Patrick Henry to his brother-in-law William Christian in 1770 as a reward for Christian's Revolutionary War service. In 1892, Lamon Harkness, a carriage-horse breeder, purchased 400 acres of the land and established Walnut Hall. The farm, which has grown and evolved since then, remains a noted Standardbred nursery that is still family-owned.

Raised on Walnut Hall's plush green pastures, Getaway Hall was sold at the Tattersalls September yearling sale in Lexington for a respectable $30,000 to Seymour Pinewski. The promising young horse was hauled across country to Pinewski's Denim Stables in New York to begin training for his racing career, but he didn't dwell there long. He passed through the hands of three subsequent owners over the next three and a half years, ending up at Pompano Park in Florida. It was there, in March 2000, that Getaway Hall caught the eye of well-known harness-horse owner Bill Brooks, better known outside racing circles as the founder of Brooks Armored Car Service, Inc. Brooks purchased the gelding in a private sale and brought him home to Delaware.

"He was a tremendous little horse," said Kevin Sizer, a Dover, Delaware, area trainer and driver who piloted the 15.1-hand plain bay gelding almost exclusively from 2001 to 2006. "I've trained and driven a lot of racehorses," said Sizer (so many that he's hard pressed even to estimate the exact number), "but he's my favorite of all time." The horse's race history explains why: Those who are familiar with Thoroughbred racing and its short equine career trajectories may be astonished to learn that Getaway Hall raced for eleven years — unusually long even by harness-racing standards — with 248 total starts. He amassed forty-nine wins, thirty-nine seconds, and nineteen third-place finishes for career earnings of nearly $697,000. In a sport in which the average horse earns $40,000 to $50,000 per year, according to Sizer, Getaway Hall's record far exceeds the norm.

Getaway Hall is "what you would call an old work horse," said Bob Brooks, a fellow harness-racing trainer out of Chesapeake City, Maryland, and the son of Bill Brooks.

Although the gelding earned a more-than-respectable amount of money during his racing career, he was not raced at the top levels of the sport, according to Bob Brooks. Instead of scoring big-money wins in fewer and more prestigious races, Getaway Hall successfully campaigned in second-tier events, making up through quantity what his races lacked in quality, especially purse size.

In Getaway Hall's career best, a 2002 race in Canada, Sizer sensed that "it was the right race" — that the horse "didn't have to have anything go his way, and he would win anyway." And win Getaway Hall did, pacing a mile in 1:50, the fastest time of the horse's career, with Sizer in the sulky. That year would prove to be Getaway Hall's top money-earner as well, with the gelding collecting a total of more than $156,500 in purses.

The elder Brooks owned Getaway Hall until December 2005, when the horse changed hands in a claiming race. In April 2006, as his career was slowly winding down, Getaway Hall was then bought by his present owner of record, Marcos Ameralis of Bergenfield, New Jersey. To secure the future of his old equine friend, Sizer purchased his former partner in spring 2008 for $1,000. According to Sizer, however, he never received the horse's papers from Ameralis, who is still listed as the current owner on Getaway Hall's United States Trotting Association (USTA) Horse Performance Report.

One would never expect a horse with such a long and solid racing history as Getaway Hall's to wind up loose along a roadside, with his owner of record nowhere to be found. But that's what happened, and that's the point at which this ex-racer's story takes a couple of unexpected turns.

Neither Sizer nor Brooks knows for sure how Getaway got away from the stable in Townsend, Delaware, where Sizer boarded him (and, yes, Brooks promptly dubbed him "Gotaway," a nickname that the Delaware news media relished). Neither man suspects abandonment or foul play: Brooks pointed out that the gelding, although his weight was down by 100 pounds or so from his normal 800-to-900 range, "looked all right when he was found; I've certainly seen horses racing that looked worse." Given that the horse was wearing a halter and a lead rope when he got loose, Sizer speculated that Getaway Hall may simply have pulled away

Getaway Hall raced 248 times — an impressive number of starts.

from his handler ("maybe a small child"), who for whatever reason couldn't or didn't catch the ex-racer.

What's known is that Getaway Hall wandered about five miles from home before being rounded up. Will Kirkwood, a Townsend horseman who identified the gelding from his tattoo, took him in until his owner could be found. A wild goose chase to track down the owner of record, Ameralis, ensued. He proved impossible to contact, with a disconnected phone number, and no one suspected he was not the true owner of the horse.

While that ultimately fruitless search was going on, word of Getaway Hall's escapade and Kirkwood's unplanned equine acquisition spread via the harness-horsemen's grapevine to trainer Adrian Wisher, who trains harness racers in Galena, Maryland. Wisher, a friend of Sizer's, remembered the horse and contacted Sizer, who was racing at Pocono Downs in Wilkes-Barre, Pennsylvania, as he does each summer.

Sizer dispatched Wisher to collect Getaway Hall, who spent a night at Wisher's farm before being moved to Bob Brooks' eighty-acre small-scale training facility in Chesapeake City. Because Sizer lacks a farm of his own, Brooks generously allowed Getaway Hall to reside free of charge with the more than forty other horses on his farm.

With an acre-and-a-half paddock all to himself, Getaway Hall is pasture sound, but "I don't think he'd be sound enough to be a riding horse," Brooks said. Called in to check out a big left hind ankle after the gelding was recovered, Brooks's veterinarian found an old injury. "I don't know exactly what happened to him," Brooks said. "At first, the vet thought it might have been a stifle injury."

Regardless, Getaway Hall is consigned to pasture-ornament status for life: He's comfortable enough to wander the fields and graze, but exercise aggravates the old injury.

Neither Sizer nor Brooks seems too concerned about reconstructing the chain of events that led to Getaway Hall's roadside wanderings, and both men are convinced the horse's previous owner is out of the picture. "I'm not worried that the owner will ever show up and claim him," Brooks said. "I think Kevin did buy the horse from the guy and never had the papers transferred." Sizer corroborates the story. "I acquired the horse but never received registration papers from that man," he said.

Thanks to the caring and generosity of Sizer, Brooks, and their colleagues, Getaway Hall is safe. But his story has a bit of a Black Beauty theme about it: Any horse's fate is uncertain, determined largely by its owner's actions. Getaway Hall's USTA report lists eleven prior owners or lessees, not including Sizer. That's an aver-

Driver Kevin Sizer called Getaway Hall a "tremendous little horse."

age of a new owner or lessee almost every fourteen months. Each change of hands — for any horse — is an opportunity for its life to take a turn for better or for worse.

Getaway Hall's story is a cautionary tale that even racehorses of esteemed origin, earning almost three-quarters of a million dollars can end up worthless (at least on paper) and unwanted. Many such castaways meet an end much sadder than Getaway Hall's. The harness-racing industry produces many Getaway Halls, Standardbreds in varying states of soundness that need good homes when their profitable racing days are over. The USTA, aware of the issue, publishes information about the Standardbred breed and links to Standardbred-adoption agencies on its Web site, www.ustrotting.com (click on "Adopt a Standardbred"). A number of ex-racing Standardbreds wind up in Amish homes, where their driving skills are put to use pulling buggies; but those outlets are, of course, limited in number.

Caring horseman that Sizer may be, he's busy training and driving the twenty Standardbred racehorses in his care and relies on the generosity of Brooks to house Getaway Hall. As a result, both Sizer and Brooks would ultimately like to find the gelding a good, permanent home.

"If you know anyone looking for a retired racehorse … " quips Sizer, in a sentiment echoed by Brooks. Hearing that the interviewer is in the market for a dressage horse, Brooks eagerly volunteers his daughter's sale horse, a young Warmblood, and quips: "Buy him and I'll throw in Getaway Hall for free!" But horse lovers needn't worry: Even if no adopter comes forward, "we'll certainly do the right thing by him," Brooks says of the gelding.

Contemplating the sheer number of unwanted horses and other animals that need homes can be overwhelming and distressing. The story of Getaway Hall is an antidote of sorts: an example of how one (or two, or a few) people can make all the difference in a horse's life, enabling a deserving old campaigner to live out his days comfortably. And in a world in which harsh economic realities force many animal owners to make difficult choices concerning their four-legged friends, it's all the more heartwarming to learn about the getaway horse whose people got him back for good.

Race Record						
YEAR	AGE	STS	1ST	2ND	3RD	EARNED
1997	at 2	7	1	1	2	$15,008
1998	at 3	25	6	3	3	$32,580
1999	at 4	39	8	7	1	$78,495
2000	at 5	21	6	4	1	$66,090
2001	at 6	30	7	6	2	$115,220
2002	at 7	24	9	1	0	$156,524
2003	at 8	27	4	7	4	$98,795
2004	at 9	23	3	3	2	$62,655
2005	at 10	25	2	2	1	$33,482
2006	at 11	25	3	5	3	$36,895
2007	at 12	2	0	0	1	$865
Lifetime		**248**	**49**	**39**	**19**	**$696,609**

Hapsirishpub

By Alexandra Beckstett

9

In a small, dark, yet authentically Irish bar in Cincinnati, Ohio, Thoroughbred owners and post-race crowds gather for drinks. At first glance Hap's Irish Pub looks like your classic watering hole, but amidst the dartboards and Celtic paraphernalia lining the walls is a photo of a robust chestnut racehorse in all his glory. Caked in mud and sweat, he leads by half a length in his final career win. Search the bar some more, and you'll discover a donation jar bearing a similar picture. The name under the horse reads Hapsirishpub, but the luck of the Irish hasn't always been on his side.

"Haps" was born in April 2000 at owner Patrick Connaire's small Thoroughbred breeding farm outside Cincinnati. Connaire frequented Hap's Irish Pub and was a good friend of its owner, Danny Thomas. It came as no surprise, therefore, when Connaire named the bright chestnut gelding in honor of Thomas' popular establishment.

On the track Haps was nothing to brag about, but unlike countless other horses bred for racing, he was someone's pet. Out of Celtic Issues and sired by graded stakes winner Count the Time, he was destined to race for several years and then retire to live out his life as an ornament in Connaire's pasture. All those close to the owner knew the horse would never leave his farm.

Trained by Ramon Salcedo, Haps ran in small 5- and 6-furlong claiming races across Ohio and was a regular at River Downs and Beulah Park. His record reveals that he was highly inconsistent and if he didn't win, he typically finished toward the back of the field. By 2005 the stress of racing had begun to take its toll on Haps' fetlock joints, and he developed sesamoid problems. Out of twenty-four starts, he had five wins and at the time of his injury had earned just over $16,600.

In late 2005 Haps' world turned upside down. Connaire passed away unexpectedly after suffering a stroke, leaving no mention of his horses in his will. As part of Connaire's estate, the ten horses that he owned at the time passed into the hands of his second wife, who in the ten or fifteen years she was married to the racing en-thusiast had never become involved with the horses. She sold all those that were fit for racing and gave Haps, laid up with the injury, to Connaire's son, Mark. Mark had lofty visions of the gelding's becoming a profitable racehorse after his recovery. To get Haps back on the track after more than a year of rest, he gave him to Pat, another Thoroughbred owner, trainer, and a close friend of his late father, with the assumption that the horse was in good hands. When, by August 2007, however, Haps would not remain sound for racing, Pat wanted him gone. Fast.

Meanwhile, in Harrison County, Kentucky, a middle-aged con-crete worker named Doug had recently relocated from Delaware to take up residence with his fiancée on property owned by his parents. He had never owned a horse before, but when he discov-

Hapsirishpub on the road to recovery after a dramatic rescue

ered through word of mouth that a horse called Hapsirishpub was being given away at River Downs, he suddenly took an interest. On a whim he drove up to look at Haps — who was handsome, healthy, and fit from months of training — and to meet Pat. Pat did not know Doug, did not ask about his horse experience or his plans for Haps, but handed him the unwanted gelding with his Coggins papers and walked away. Unbeknownst to him, Pat had just given his late friend's beloved horse to a stranger with severe mental problems.

Haps' new owner gave no consideration to the fact that he did not have the land, facilities, or money to care for a horse. He simply brought him home and shut him out of sight in an old hog barn, empty of animals but thick with manure and littered with rusting farm equipment. For seven months Haps lived in the dark, putrid barn without exercise, sunshine, or care. During this period,

Kentucky experienced a drought that drove hay prices sky high. When Doug didn't want to pay for the pricey hay, his solution was to stop feeding Haps altogether. His concerned fiancée, an animal-lover at heart who raised chickens, used what little funds she had from selling eggs to help Haps. She was able to buy just enough horse feed to keep the deteriorating Thoroughbred alive.

As Doug's mental demons continued to plague him, his fiancée tried to reach out to his friends and family for help. She received neither reply nor relief and feared for her own safety. She was afraid that if she were to seek help for Haps as well, Doug might harm her. In her mind, she was powerless. In March 2008, Doug reached his breaking point. He took his own life, leaving behind a penniless, pregnant fiancée and a starving horse. The fiancée contacted local animal control officers, who in turn called Shelly Price, co-founder of Speak Up for Horses, a Kentucky-based equine rescue and rehabilitation organization, to help with the horse she had grown to love but could not afford to maintain.

Price recalled the pathetic sight that greeted her when she arrived at the farm: "I slid the barn door open and could barely even see him in the dark," she said. What she could make out was a severely malnourished horse standing in deep manure, his body covered in sores and his feet so overgrown they curled up in front.

"He had a terrible wound on his right hind leg below his hock, but I couldn't tell what it was. I just knew there was something really bad encased in all that dirt and crust. Above the wound was this gap that ran up his leg between the skin and meat. We assume he cut himself on the farm machinery," said Price.

How long Haps' wounds had gone unnoticed no one is sure, but

Malnutrition left Hapsirishpub so weak he could barely move.

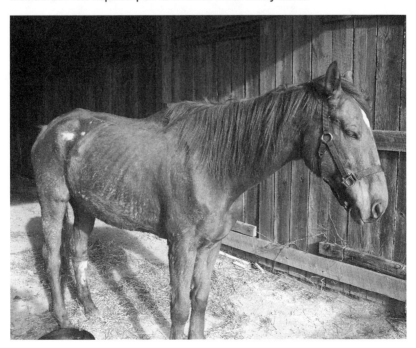

he was found dehydrated, without food, and with only a small amount of foul water — just enough to keep him alive. The 16.2-hand horse should have weighed around twelve hundred pounds but scaled a mere eight hundred.

Price's initial concern was just getting Haps onto the horse trailer and off the property. He could only hobble a few feet out of the dark barn before pain and fatigue brought him to a halt. But Haps slowly worked his way to the trailer and stepped up into it without hesitation. He knew what he needed to do to save himself.

Doug's fiancée had signed the ownership for Haps over to Price, who accepted the daunting task of cleaning him up and nursing him back to health. She did not, however, have an open stall at her Falmouth, Kentucky, farm, so Haps was transported to the farm of her friend and neighbor, Mike Patterson. Patterson and his wife, Kelly, had several rescue horses of their own and could provide Haps with temporary housing. There, doctors Paul Garofolo and Dale Beighle of Grants Lick Veterinary Hospital in Butler, Kentucky, arrived to examine the horse. Through blood work they were able to determine that the starvation had not yet affected his internal organs. Rescuers had reached him in the nick of time. Haps did, however, have extremely bruised feet, the worst Price had ever seen.

"No one really knows how it happened. The soles of his feet were just one massive bruise," said Price. The manure in the hog barn was so thick that rescuers were unable to tell what lay beneath it and what might have caused the bruising. It was evident though that walking was incredibly painful for Haps.

For nearly three weeks Price commuted from her farm to the Pattersons' several times a day to feed, groom, and care for Haps. It was both time-consuming and physically and emotionally draining.

"You know, it's hard to brush bones," she said. "It was so deep between his ribs that I had to use the brush on the back of a hoof pick to get the dirt and manure out."

By mid-April a stall opened up in Price's barn and Haps could be relocated. He continued to undergo a rigorous treatment of immune boosters, antibiotics, and tetanus shots. Because Haps had not had a fresh bale of hay in more than three months, his digestive system could only handle very low-quality hay. He would have to be slowly and carefully reintroduced to forage. He also began receiving massage therapy from TLC Equine therapist Teresa Bossow for the muscles that had atrophied from not being used in seven months.

"His muscles were so sore that I couldn't brush his back end," said Price. "If I used the lightest brush on his rump, he would drop it a couple inches to get away."

Furthermore, Haps was so weak and his muscles so debilitated that swinging his front legs out to the side when he walked was easier than picking them up and moving forward. According to Price, he looked like a duck when he walked — a far cry from the strapping racehorse he used to be.

Haps was so frail from months of being immobilized in the hog barn that, initially, he could not be turned out in the pasture. Price hand walked him two or three times each day to get him moving and building muscle. As Haps grew stronger, he slowly began moving less like a duck and more like a horse.

When he was rescued in March, Haps still sported a thick winter coat that masked the true extent of his condition. Not only was he thinner than he looked under all the hair, but when he started shedding, large parts of his shoulders, face, and rump were completely bald.

Price was shocked, and Dr. Beighle just shook his head. "Starvation affects a lot of things," he said.

In addition to Haps' poor physical condition, Price and Dr. Beighle were concerned about his mental state. "Fortunately, he was eating, but he was depressed. It was as if he had given up and wouldn't get the fight back," said Price.

Unaccustomed to his new lifestyle, Haps would stand all day in his stall with his head in the corner. He never gazed out the stall window or greeted Price when she entered the barn. After about three weeks, however, as Price walked down her driveway, Haps stuck his head out the window for the first time and whinnied. Price didn't know whether to laugh or cry.

"Well, he's back," she said.

Naturally, mounting expenses accompanied Price's tireless efforts to rehabilitate Haps. To help raise funds, the local news channel aired a segment documenting his rescue and recovery. It turned out that through his racing career and connection to the pub, Haps was, in fact, well known and admired in the Cincinnati area. Word about his situation got back to former owner Pat, who in an attempt to redeem himself in the eyes of Haps' followers, called Price and offered to take the horse.

"I just laughed," said Price, astounded that a man who threw Haps away with no consideration for the horse's well being would ask to have him back. "I asked, 'Did you know the guy you gave Haps to? No. Did you ask him any questions? No. You just wanted to dump him and you won't get him back.' "

Having been made aware of Haps' plight, pub owner Danny Thomas also became extremely upset. In the horse's honor he hosted "Hapsirishpub night at Hap's Irish Pub," a small benefit for the horse whose win photo still hangs upon his wall. Thomas also made a personal visit to Price's farm to see how his old friend's horse was doing.

Throughout 2008, Haps continued to receive monthly massage therapy to help with his strength and recovery, but the process remained slow.

"He has good days and bad days," Price admitted seven months after his rescue. "Some days he still seems lame or he will swing his legs out to the side. His wound is also still in the process of healing and he needs about one hundred more pounds of weight on him."

But Price has fallen in love with the expressive chestnut face that greets her when she walks through the barn each day. Both she and Haps' veterinarians see no reason why he shouldn't end up sound for riding and enjoy a new career with Price.

"He is the most wonderful horse that you would ever want to meet," said Price. "People come and see him that have heard his story. He loves everybody and doesn't have a mean bone in his body. He's a sweet, sweet boy."

Fittingly renamed "Happy," the lanky Thoroughbred joins Price's hodgepodge of equine rescues that she has amassed over the years, from her retired dressage mount to a leopard Appaloosa to an ornery old pony that no one else wanted. While Price's twenty-four-year-old Thoroughbred gelding, Darmonte, another ex-racehorse rescued from a kill buyer's truck, runs each day in the pasture like he's back on the track, Happy is still content to walk. Not yet ready for the run and chase of the "new guy" with Price's other horses, he goes out each day by himself. Price and Dr. Beighle have noticed that Happy does not roll like horses normally do when turned out. It's a reminder that he still has quite a way to go before his body no longer hurts.

Although Happy was born into great care, owned by a man who loved his horses and treated them like family, his story is a lesson in preparedness.

"People that have horses need to prepare for the future, because you never know," said a solemn Price. "You always figure if you get sick, you'll make plans then. "

After all he's been through, Happy can rest assured that he will always have a safe place in Price's barn, not to mention her heart.

On the chilly morning of December 1, 2008, Happy finally felt like a real horse again. For the first time in more than a year he galloped across a field, bucking and playing with a youthful exuberance Price once thought was lost. She watched as he snorted and ran with tail held high around his pasture. He was completely sound.

Race and (Stakes) Record

YEAR	AGE	STS	1ST	2ND	3RD	EARNED
2003	at 3	7	0 (0)	0 (0)	0 (0)	$881
2004	at 4	8	3 (0)	0 (0)	0 (0)	$9,368
2005	at 5	9	2 (0)	0 (0)	0 (0)	$6,354
Lifetime		**24**	**5 (0)**	**0 (0)**	**0 (0)**	**$16,603**

Kona

By Sherry Pinson

10

To understand this story, you will have to set aside logic and practicality and prudence. You will have to forget what you know about balanced books, bottom lines, and common sense.

Instead you will have to believe in extravagance, long odds, serendipity, and maybe even a little magic.

In a trader's lot in the state of Washington in June 2005, a cattle truck stood with its metal door rolled up and its ramp down. The truck had been hired by a Canadian slaughterhouse and it periodically made the rounds of lots like this one, gathering up horses — not cattle — that were used up, unwanted, or simply too numerous for the local market to absorb. The deal was struck, an ordinary business deal trading money for goods, and the horses were herded toward the ramp.

A big, dark bay mare with two hind socks stood among the others, waiting her turn to load, one of many whose names no longer mattered.

Now in her mid-fifties, Paula Drake is a reasonable woman, well educated. When decisions must be made, she is practical and thorough, careful to consider requirements and consequences. Her current job as a researcher with the Cincinnati office of the county auditor suits her well. At one time she bred and sold Akita puppies, and her sensible approach proved a boon to clients who otherwise would succumb to puppy charm first and only later realize the practicalities. She advised them to research various breeds carefully and consider how each would fit their lifestyles. She recommended they visit the breeder and meet their prospective puppy's parents before making a decision. Such a careful, considered approach to animal ownership offered the best promise of a good match, she advised.

Then, in 1980, Paula decided to buy her first horse. "I had always loved horses," she said. "I had ridden off and on for years and always wanted one of my own."

Her knowledge of horses provided a foundation for the decision, but when she met the Appaloosa named Comanche, her reasoned approach wrestled with that inexplicable pull horses have on the heart. Research? It was hard to come by; Comanche had been left behind by a boarder who skipped town, and Paula was his fifth owner in six years. A good match? She wanted a riding horse; Comanche hated a saddle.

Her heart won out. "I found myself in a place where there was no one to tell me I couldn't do it," she recalled. "So I bought Comanche for $500."

"I rode him bareback until he learned to trust me," Paula said. "There were lots of past training issues to overcome. By trial and error I discovered he loved the trails, and he adored my four-year-old daughter. So I put her up behind me and we raced around the cornfields of our farm for the first few months."

Paula owned Comanche until 2002, when she sold her small farm east of Cincinnati. By then Comanche was nearly blind, and no public boarding barn would take him. Finally, she placed him with a friend of a friend who had an equally aged blind mare. Comanche died in his sleep about six months later.

Adjusting to life without her companion of twenty-two years, Paula eventually heeded friends who urged her to keep riding. She took lessons in dressage for the next two years, riding her instructor's retired show horse. But Comanche's death had left a hole in her life, and her heart ached for another horse of her own.

By the time she began her search in 2004, horse sellers and horse buyers had begun to connect via the Internet. Seeking another Appaloosa, Paula checked Web sites offering horses for sale. She stumbled onto *The Chronicle of the Horse*, and from threads on its bulletin board discovered the other side of buying and selling horses: trader lots and slaughterhouses. One particular incident, an accident involving a double-decker rig that overturned on an Indiana highway, ate at her tender heart. Of the fifty horses on board that September afternoon in 2004, at least twenty-one had died as a result of the accident. Where had they come from? Some had braided manes and painted hooves; who had so recently loved them and dressed them up? What became of those that survived? What was this business of selling horses to slaughterhouses?

As Paula learned more about this darker side of horse-trading, she also learned about rescue operations. And eventually she discovered the trader lot in the state of Washington, more than 2,000 miles away, where the big, dark bay mare with the two hind socks would one day line up for the cattle truck bound for Canada.

Formed in August 2004, a small group calling itself Columbia Basin Equine Rescue (CBER) had established a relationship with the owner of the lot in Washington. The owner had a contract with a Canadian slaughterhouse, but he didn't care where his profits came from. If the rescue group got money together, he would separate out the horses they bought until they could transport them to a local foster facility. He would even hold horses they were still working to redeem, to a point; if a contract truck from Canada happened to come along, only horses fully paid for by the rescue group were safe. Once boarded on a truck bound for the slaughterhouse's holding facility in Stanwood, Washington, a horse was out of reach.

CBER sought funds by posting online photos of horses they were trying to save, and a group of people connected through forums on *The Chronicle of the Horse* Web site began to pool their money. In addition to Paula, the group included several women from the Pacific Northwest area, a woman from Palo Alto, California, another from Toronto, one from Charleston, South Carolina; and a woman from Tennessee. None had met face to face.

"You would see the typical comments about the postings," said Paula. " 'Oh, isn't she beautiful?' 'Does anybody know anyone who would want her?' 'His price is only $200.' 'Oh, let's not forget about this one.' So our group started making a list of CBER horses we wanted our money to rescue."

The big, dark bay mare with the two hind socks had come in to the Washington lot with several other horses, including two older mares. The rescue group described the bay as a Thoroughbred, fifteen to twenty years old, "gorgeous, with lovely conformation." The report noted recent injuries, a gash from a kick and an abrasion, both suffered at the trader lot. She was nervous at being in the lot, the posting said, and she was wary of men. Because of her size, she was listed at $800.

Her name was Kona, and she became Paula's cause. "We've got to get this one out," she told the group.

"Kona wasn't very high on the list," Paula recalled. "The two other mares who came in with her were about the same age, but they were higher up — I don't know why."

One by one, as money came in, horses higher on the list moved to the safe holding pen. Kona did not.

Finally enough money came in to rescue Kona, and the rescue worker headed to the lot. But the truck from Canada had shown up earlier than usual, on a Sunday, and the deal with the slaughterhouse buyer had already been made. Kona was already in line, ready to load.

The worker pleaded with the lot owner; she had cash in hand for this exact mare, this very one, she told him. Because of her size, he countered that she was worth more than the others. Finally, the owner agreed to let Kona leave the line, but as the rescuer led the big mare away, she watched in horror as two other horses were loaded in Kona's place.

Shortly thereafter, in late June 2005, Kona and several others were moved to a foster home in Elma, Washington, one of several facilities that had opened to help with the growing number of rescues bought off the trader's lot. One by one, the horses rescued with Kona were adopted. Once again, Kona was left behind.

"I had no intention of adopting Kona," Paula said, a wry smile lighting her face as she recalled her own advice to puppy buyers. "I'd never touched her. I'd never ridden her. I'd never even seen her move. I didn't know anything about her — no one did. But there she was, waiting and waiting. My friends said, 'Paula! Kona's sitting out there for a reason.'

"There were closer lots, other horses I could buy, but by that point I was asking myself, 'How am I going to do this? What about the logistics?' A young girl had visited Kona and was sort of interested in her, so I decided that if she took Kona, that was it — that would be as it should be.

"But the girl walked away. I knew then that Kona was meant to be mine."

Friends of the rescue operation found a driver who would, for a reasonable fee, add two rescues to a scheduled haul, and in September 2005, after a meandering, ten-day, cross-country trip, Kona arrived at a boarding farm east of Cincinnati and not far from Paula's home.

Kona was already thin when she left the trader lot, and a drought that summer in the Elma area further compromised her weight. By the time she got to Paula, every rib was visible. She had traveled cross-country in a slant-load trailer that was too small for her, and over the long journey she developed two football-sized hematomas on her rump, one on each side of her tail. But as she finally stepped off the trailer, her eyes were bright with curiosity and a sense of adventure. She whirled and kicked and bucked at the end of her long line, seeming to celebrate that she'd seen the last of the slant-load. Lingering stiffness from her confinement worked itself out over the

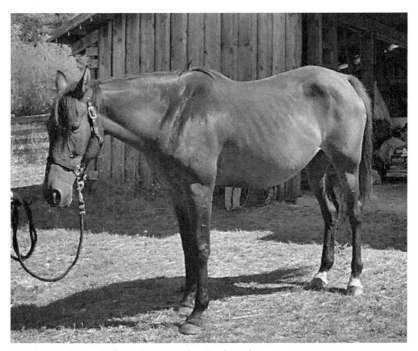

Kona's ribs showed when she arrived at Paula's place.

following few days, and she rebounded quickly under Paula's care. "She was perfectly happy in her new environment from the start," Paula said.

When Kona left Washington, she had been brand-inspected as required by law. An earlier attempt to read her tattoo had produced only a guess. The markings were faded and uneven, some mere dots after so many years. Maybe the tattoo began with an "O"; that would make her twenty, born in 1986. At the brand inspection, more practiced eyes discovered an "R" before the "O." She was eighteen, foaled in 1988.

As Kona recovered, Paula doggedly worked to decipher the tattoo. "I looked at it from all angles, with a flashlight, without a flashlight, with blacklights, on digital photos. One by one most of the

119

numbers became clearer. What we thought was an 'O' was a zero, the first of her numbers. Eventually, I had enough to contact The Jockey Club, and after a couple of tries and with the help of a sympathetic researcher, we got a match."

Kona was Cassal Pond. She had a name, a history, and a trail.

By Cassaleria out of Treasure Pond, Cassal Pond was a homebred owned by Guy and Barbara Roberts and foaled March 30, 1988, on their Guy Bar Farm in Washington. She raced sixteen times, nine at Longacres and seven at Playfair, both Washington tracks long since closed. In her third start, a mile at Longacres on September 13, 1990, she broke her maiden by a six-length margin. At Playfair later that fall she won the Juvenile Mile-Hers Stakes and was second in the Spokane Futurity. She finished her racing career with three wins, one second, and earnings of $33,388. Retired from racing in 1991, Cassal Pond produced six foals for Guy Roberts and Guy Bar Farm, all of them winners.

Cassal Pond also aborted a foal in 1996, and from 2001 through 2005 her breeding record shows either no report or failure to conceive.

Now eighty years old, Guy Roberts has spent his entire career breeding and racing Thoroughbreds. He is well regarded for his horsemanship and commitment to Washington racing and in 1998 was appointed to the Washington State Racing Commission, serving two years. At its peak in the 1990s, Guy Bar Farm owned more than thirty-five broodmares and stood five stallions, including Petersburg, a son of Danzig.

A father of five, many times a grandfather and great-grandfather, Guy Roberts is a family man and Guy Bar Farm is a family business. But business had to be the operative word, and culling unproductive horses was part of it. Guy kept Cassal Pond through five barren seasons, trying repeatedly to get her in foal even though he knew that her previous failures to conceive meant she likely would never conceive again. Eventually, though, he conceded to reality and arranged to send her to the trader.

"I try really hard not to be judgmental and point fingers," said Paula. "The bottom line is that this is Kona's story, not the story of the trader who made two others go in her place, and not the story of a business decision to sell her to the trader."

In fact, Paula said, she "put aside any prejudice" and wrote Guy "a letter from the heart." The two struck up a friendly correspondence.

"I grew to understand that he held onto Kona as long as he did because she was special to him," said Paula. "He told me he had no idea anyone would want an old broodmare." To this day, Paula and Guy keep in touch.

Through the fall of 2005, Kona continued to recover, and Paula began riding her. "She was perfect," Paula said. "Except for the girl who first considered adopting her, she hadn't been ridden in fifteen years, but she was eager, willing, and thrilling to ride. I finally found a horse that fit my long legs! We had the best of times through Christmas that year and I began to make plans to show her in 2006."

Kona was not an easy keeper. She was fit, muscling up, but still lean despite three full plates a day. In January, Paula noticed the mare had gained some weight, but it seemed to be settling across her belly. Later that belly began filling out to the sides, and the once agile mare began, as Paula describes it, "galumping around the arena like a walrus."

Kona, the eighteen-year-old mare who couldn't conceive, was pregnant.

Sent from the only home she had ever known, stressed by the chaos of the trader lot, shuttled from pen to pen to foster care, exposed to who knows what, debilitated by drought and her long journey, with no supplemental nutrition, and older besides, still she held onto the foal.

A miracle, Paula's vet pronounced.

A victory against long odds, a bit of serendipity, maybe even magic.

With an ultrasound confirming that Kona had to have conceived before she was shipped to the trader lot, Paula called Guy Roberts.

"It was quite an interesting phone call," Paula said. "He said, 'Well, I'll be ... oh, my, oh, my.' He felt some regret, he said, but he was happy for Kona and for me. 'I'll make good,' he said, 'no problem. That's a Petersburg baby. Yep, here's her cover date. Yep, you're going to have yourself a fine baby.'"

Earlier matings of Kona and Petersburg had produced Peter's Pond, an eighteen-time winner with earnings of more than a quarter-million dollars, and Capable of Gold, a four-time winner. Counting this miracle pregnancy, Roberts had tried three other times to get another Petersburg foal from Kona. After her last cover, he'd left the job of ultrasounds to a new barn manager. Was Kona missed? Was the reading incorrect? No one knows.

Given her broodmare's belly, she had been palpated on arrival at the rescue facility. The pregnancy was missed there, too.

On April 21, 2006, Kona delivered a dark bay filly. Although registered as Dancing on Dreams, the filly is called Lucy, meaning "of first light."

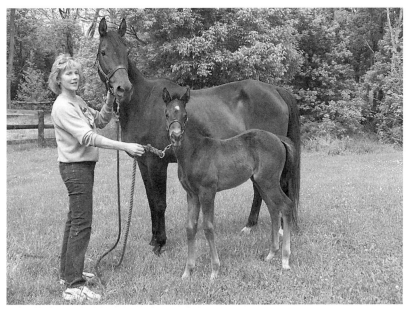

Paula proudly shows off Kona and her foal, Lucy.

Five weeks after foaling, Kona colicked, always a risk with an older mare and especially when the foal is large, as Lucy was. At Hagyard Equine Medical Center in Lexington, Kentucky, Kona improved when her displaced colon righted itself. She was even allowed outside to hand-graze with Lucy beside her, and Paula snapped photo after photo of the two of them together.

But the colon slipped again, hepatitis set in, and Kona was lost.

Paula was devastated, and Lucy was adrift. Dr. Nathan Slovis, an internist at Hagyard, insisted that Lucy should see and smell that her mother was dead; otherwise, she would have a harder time accepting the absence of her mother and might not thrive. Even now, tears pour down Paula's face when she recalls the little filly snuffling and nosing at the mother who could not respond.

Back at the boarding stable, despite all efforts, Lucy slid into depression. She would not drink milk from a bucket. She played with water in a bucket and knew how to drink, but she would not drink the milk she needed.

Desperate to save her miracle baby, Paula called on a friend from Last Chance Corral near Athens, Ohio, a facility that rescues nurse mare foals. Ten days later a sorrel colt about Lucy's age arrived, a "maybe Saddlebred-something cross," all legs and mischief.

"We had a 'Lucy,'" Paula said. "What else could we call him but 'Desi'?"

Desi had been handled very little and had no use for a halter. He was rowdy and rambunctious; had he been human, he'd have had a cowlick and a gap-toothed grin. At first sight of him, Lucy did the only sensible thing; she hid. But within forty-eight hours they were fast friends, and Lucy followed Desi's lead right into the milk bucket.

Desi and Lucy are best friends.

Today, at two, Lucy and Desi are still best friends. They face each other across the aisle at the boarding barn, and in the field they move as one. He's still a handful, "a punk," Paula said; you can almost hear him say, "Hey, Luce, c'mon! C'mon, let's play. *Luuuce ... come on!*" Lucy indulges and mothers him. Except that she has a star and no hind socks, she is her mother all over again, big of body but elegant, dark, and lean. Her trot is liquid, her movements well balanced. She stands with an innate sense of self, her intelligence obvious.

Paula's impractical, illogical, long-distance adoption of one aging mare laid the foundation for a legacy. Because she adopted Kona, Paula also rescued Lucy. Discarded as worthless, Desi proved invaluable to Lucy's survival and found a home where he is treasured. Because she still needed a riding horse and had come to appreciate older horses, Paula also adopted Bernard's Choice, a nineteen-year-old former racehorse renamed Elliott By God. At every step, new human friendships blossomed.

Kona's legacy now writes a larger story. Grieving over Kona's death and well versed in the plight of unwanted horses, Paula joined a like-minded friend, Shelly Price, to establish Speak Up for Horses in 2006. A registered nonprofit based in Kentucky, Speak Up for Horses focuses on education. The group teaches law enforcement agencies and county elected officials to recognize equine abuse and neglect, works to ensure enforcement of laws already on the books, and champions stronger animal protection legislation where needed. Speak Up for Horses also offers seminars on horse ownership, so horses get a head start with owners who know what to expect and how to choose wisely. The dream down the road includes a facility for more hands-on instruction.

"We've been involved in several rescues, but we're not a rescue *per se* because we don't have a farm," said Paula. "The fact is, you can rescue 'til the cows come home, but simply rescuing horses in need is not enough. We must root out the *need* for rescue through education and good example.

"We are responsible to leave a legacy of compassion and respect. The lessons learned in owning and caring for horses translate to how we care for our environment and how we treat our fellow human beings.

"For whatever fateful reason, Kona chose me to care for her final foal. The hard realities will probably always be there to fight, but Lucy and I will dance on dreams together, with Kona's sweet spirit ever lighting the way."

Race and (Stakes) Record

YEAR	AGE	STS	1ST	2ND	3RD	EARNED
1990	at 2	8	2 (0)	1 (0)	0 (0)	$31,913
1991	at 3	8	1 (0)	0 (0)	0 (0)	$1,475
Lifetime		**16**	**3 (0)**	**1 (0)**	**0 (0)**	**$33,388**

LINDROS AND IMPROPRIETY

By Jennifer Morrison

Keith Brettel had never ridden a Thorough-bred before Lindros arrived at the special needs riding school at WindReach Farm in Ashburn, Ontario, in the summer of 2008. One of the more qualified student riders at WindReach, Brettel, a paraplegic, was apprehensive about being one of the first to ride the once headstrong gelding.

"I was quite nervous," remembers Brettel, who has ridden and volunteered at WindReach for half a dozen years. He had no reason for concern, though, for Lindros behaved like a perfect gentlemen. "I was delighted and surprised once I got on him; he was so professional and good at what he was doing," said Brettel.

Lindros proved so good at his job as a therapy horse that he soon became a barn favorite, enabling handicapped riders to gain confidence as equestrians. He is one of two former racehorses (the other is his paddock buddy Impropriety) used in the therapeutic riding program at WindReach, a registered charity founded by Sandy Mitchell in 1989 and encompassing more than 100 acres of farmland.

Mitchell, an accomplished horseman with cerebral palsy who has ridden in the equestrian events at the Paralympics, introduced the therapeutic riding program at WindReach to provide people with similar disabilities the opportunity to work outdoors in a farm atmosphere.

Until 2008, the majority of the riding horses at WindReach were mixed breeds, ponies and horses carefully purchased for their gentle nature.

That is until WindReach's stable manager and instructor Laura Ireland took a chance and adopted Lindros and Impropriety from the LongRun Thoroughbred Retirement Foundation. For Lindros in particular, the journey that brought him to WindReach had its

Keith Brettel remembers feeling nervous when he first rode Lindros.

But Keith quickly found out he had nothing to fear.

share of ironic twists and turns for he had been intended for great things on the racetrack.

Indeed, Lindros was saddled with lofty expectations as soon as his breeders, Punch and Anne Kent, named the bay colt after the famous National Hockey League star Eric Lindros.

A son of Kentucky Derby winner Strike the Gold out of the stakes-winning mare Chateau d'Irlande, Lindros was foaled at the Kents' Hope Stock Farm in Port Stanley, Ontario, in 1997.

As a yearling, the colt was sold for $23,044 (U.S.) through consignor Charlene Smith to Ron Connelly. The following year, 1999, Lindros went through the auction ring at the Ocala March two-year-old in training sale, where Canadian trainer Mike DePaulo purchased him for Toronto native Roger Patten. "We were looking for a Queen's Plate horse," said DePaulo, referring to the most prestigious race in Canada. "He was a good-looking horse and most importantly, a Canadian-bred. So we paid $40,000 (U.S.) for him."

It did not take Lindros long to parlay his good looks and promise into monetary results. He won his career debut so impressively, with a furious rush from off the pace in a 5½-furlong race, that offers to buy him rolled in from around the continent.

"He trained like a good horse right away," said DePaulo. "I was not surprised that he won his debut at the short distance, but his pedigree did say he wanted to go farther."

Indeed, with a Derby-winning sire and a dam that had won two stakes races at route distances, Lindros figured to have all the stamina points needed for longer races.

Despite some lucrative offers, Patten did not want to sell his prized colt, and Lindros made his next start three weeks later in the Vandal Stakes for Canadian-bred two-year-olds. Sent off at 9-5 as the second favorite, Lindros could only finish third, beaten seven lengths.

A few weeks later he would finish a flat fifth in the Simcoe Stakes at seven furlongs, deflating most of the excitement that had been generated from his career debut score.

DePaulo thinks an incident soon after Lindros' first start ultimately had an adverse affect on the colt for the remainder of his career.

"He was getting a bath one morning and he was playing around with the lead shank," said DePaulo. "He got a tooth caught on it, scared himself, and flipped over backwards. I don't think he was ever the same after that."

Lindros spent the winter of 2000 in Florida with a string of DePaulo's runners and returned to Woodbine for one of the first prep races for the Plate — the Achievement Stakes. Racing with the anti-bleeder medication Lasix for the first time, Lindros trailed through the six-furlong race and lost by twenty-two lengths.

DePaulo went back to the drawing board with Lindros, putting him in allowance races and high claiming events in the hopes of rediscovering that flash of brilliance from the colt's debut. But it would not be until November of that year before Lindros won again — a $32,000 claiming race from which he was claimed away from Patten and DePaulo.

Mike Wright Jr., a leading trainer at Woodbine, took the horse that day for Vancouver's Jerome Rak, owner of Prairie Star Stable.

Lindros became tough to handle as he matured, and Wright Jr. remembers many mornings when his exercise riders would wince when they knew it was their turn to ride the horse.

"He would put his head down, right between his knees and just go," said Wright Jr. "He was one of the toughest ones I have ever seen. Not many of my riders could get him to slow down."

The Wright Jr. barn spent the next winter at Laurel Park racecourse in Maryland, a track that quickly became a favorite surface for Lindros. Four years old and newly gelded, Lindros reeled off three consecutive wins in less than a month as he worked his way through his conditions in allowance events. A romp in a seven-furlong test over a treacherously deep surface earned him a whopping 107 Beyer Speed Figure from *Daily Racing Form*, suggesting he was one of the fastest sprinters on the continent at the time. The Speed Figure is a calculation based on running time and track condition speed, with the three-figure numbers being exceptionally good.

"I'll never forget that day," said Wright Jr. "The announcer yelled out 'and here comes Lindros; he shoots, he scores.'"

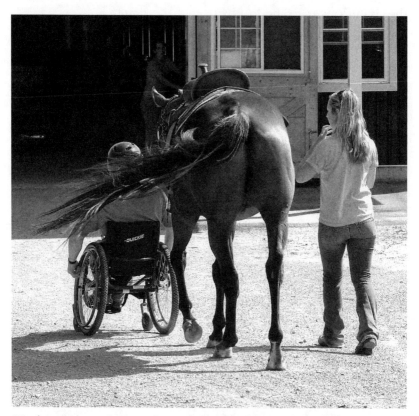

"He doesn't do anything wrong," says WindReach's Laura Ireland of Lindros.

That winter, physical wear and tear began to take their toll on Lindros, in particular on his suspensory ligaments in both front legs, and upon returning to Canada, he was sent to a swimming facility near Woodbine.

He was brought back to the races in November 2001 and won at Woodbine and Laurel through June of the following year, but the more he raced, the more his suspensories bothered him.

The last two wins of his career came in $12,500 and $20,000 claiming events before leg problems sidelined him again that summer.

"I tried to bring him back in 2003 in the spring, but he just wasn't going to hold up," said Wright Jr.

Lindros was retired with nine wins in twenty-eight starts and earnings of $198,616 (Canadian).

In May 2003, Rak donated Lindros to LongRun Thoroughbred Retirement Foundation, Ontario's only Thoroughbred adoption and placement program, and the gelding was sent to one of its foster farms run by horse owner Mary Zimmerman.

"I remember he was wound up like a top," said Zimmerman. "He was nervous and a stall walker. He just wanted to be outside. He hated being alone in the barn."

Zimmerman had Lindros only until December when a former employee, Uli Paulischta, then twenty-four years old, inquired about adopting the horse as a teaser for a Standardbred farm she was managing in Schomberg, Ontario.

For more than a year Lindros was the man in charge at White Sands Farm, and according to Paulischta, he adapted well. Lindros worked as a teaser to determine whether mares were ready to be bred and served as a companion for non-pregnant mares.

But White Sands went out of business in 2005 and Paulischta, despite having her own horse to take care of, felt obligated to take over the adoption of Lindros. She didn't do much with Lindros for the next two years, and that quiet life seemed to help him calm down. Soon, Paulischta was able to put some of her friends who wanted to learn to ride on the gelding's back.

"He lived a very quiet, very boring life," said Paulischta. "Both of my horses were just pets; they got ridden a bit, but most of the time I just fed them carrots."

In the summer of 2008, Paulischta, firmly in her new job as manager of a growing Thoroughbred farm in Orangeville, Ontario, made the tough decision that she could no longer afford to keep Lindros.

LongRun's policy is that adopters must keep a horse for two years without selling it and give LongRun the guardian rights. As Paulischta had had Lindros for more than two years, the agency was no longer responsible for him.

Paulischta contacted LongRun, hoping she could get help placing Lindros in a new home.

LongRun contacted WindReach's Laura Ireland, who had already been working with Impropriety, another LongRun graduate. After giving the horse a test ride, she liked him immediately.

"He was so calm; it was pretty neat," said Ireland, who put Lindros, re-named Bear, in lead-around lessons for her special needs students just one week after he arrived at WindReach.

"It's just amazing. It didn't take him long to be comfortable with group lessons, private lessons, grooming seminars, and being ridden western and bareback. He doesn't do anything wrong."

Lindros' Race and (Stakes) Record						
YEAR	AGE	STS	1ST	2ND	3RD	EARNED
1999	at 2	3	1 (0)	0 (0)	1 (1)	$30,645
2000	at 3	12	2 (0)	2 (0)	0 (0)	$64,552
2001	at 4	5	3 (0)	0 (0)	0 (0)	$56,190
2002	at 5	8	3 (0)	1 (0)	0 (0)	$47,229
Lifetime		**28**	**9 (0)**	**3 (0)**	**1 (1)**	**$198,616**

And Ireland found it hard to believe he was the same horse she had seen in a LongRun promotional video, running in one of his nine winning races and bouncing around headstrong on and off the track.

While Lindros was an instant hit, Ireland's other reclamation project, Impropriety, had needed several months after his arrival at WindReach in January 2008 to put on weight and acclimate to his new home.

A tall, leggy chestnut to Lindros' shorter bay guise, Impropriety raced for Edward Freeman, a LongRun board member who bought the gelding for $5,000 from breeders Gail Wood and Dr. Ruth Barbour.

He won his fifth career start in a $32,000 claiming race at Woodbine and raced in California and Fort Erie before chips in his knees curtailed his racing career.

Impropriety was retrained by Fenella Semple-Braun, a British horsewoman with five years of training horses for LongRun on her resume.

He was adopted as a riding horse by a neighbor of Semple-Braun's but returned to her farm a year later when the owner's circumstances changed.

Impropriety gives confidence to his riders.

Skinny and subdued, Impropriety was brought back to Semple-Braun's, who invited Ireland to look at the horse.

"He was very sweet. He would just put his head on your shoulder; he loves all the attention. You actually feel like he is hugging you."

Ireland's students had a contest to re-name Impropriety and the name Chance was selected "because we all thought he had been given another chance at life after racing."

Both Bear and Chance have adapted well to the quiet life at WindReach.

"It's funny; I think they know when there are children or inexperienced riders on them," said Ireland about her two ex-racehorse stars. "When I get on them, they might try to canter and have some fun."

For the special needs students of WindReach, not only is riding Bear and Chance exciting because they were once racehorses, but it is also invaluable for their physical and emotional development.

"The movement of a horse when he walks mimics that of a person's hips," said Ireland. "It gives our students so much strength in their lower body.

"They gain so much confidence high up on the horses too, they feel like they are in control of this huge animal, like they are on top of the world."

In addition to a new career, Impropriety has a new name: Chance.

Today, Bear and Chance are inseparable when turned out in the paddock together. Healthy and happy themselves, they provide the same health and happiness to their horse-loving students.

Freeman summed it up best when he said, "If you treat them well, with love and faith, they will give back."

And giving back is what Bear and Chance do best.

Impropriety's Race and (Stakes) Record

YEAR	AGE	STS	1ST	2ND	3RD	EARNED
2003	at 2	4	1 (0)	1 (0)	0 (0)	$28,114
2004	at 3	9	0 (0)	3 (0)	1 (0)	$15,457
Lifetime		**13**	**1 (0)**	**4 (0)**	**1 (0)**	**$43,571**

PHINNY

By ELIZA McGRAW

12

In 2001 a young woman named Allie Conrad left her home in Maryland with $500 in her pocket to save a horse. She was headed to Pennsylvania for the New Holland horse auction, which locals refer to as "the killer sale" because of the number of horsemeat buyers who attend. An avid rider from her early teens, Conrad had recently graduated from college. The meeting of horse and woman that followed led not only to an exceptional partnership, but also to the founding of the Communication Alliance to Network Thoroughbred Ex-Racehorses (CANTER) Mid-Atlantic, an organization determined to build similarly special relationships in riders and their off-the-track Thoroughbreds.

Although she was determined and in good spirits as she headed for the auction, Conrad found herself unprepared for the chaos she encountered at New Holland. She had expected an auction house as calm and orderly as most other horse auctions she had attended, with an auctioneer clearly stating the name, background, and attributes of each horse as it stood in front of him. But at New Holland, Conrad found, horses went through the ring in rapid-fire succession, making it difficult to take in the auctioneer's comments and distinguish one horse from another. She went to bid on a Thoroughbred she had seen and liked, but with all the confusion, it turned out that Conrad had actually bid her hard-earned $500 for a different Thoroughbred, a chestnut gelding she had not wanted.

Once Conrad went to claim him, she recognized the horse right away by his poor body condition, which she had noticed in the auction's stalls. The gelding had been standing next to a surly pony that kept kicking him. Conrad had also noticed that the horse was skinny, and that he seemed to be suffering from cellulitis, an infection that causes the legs to swell. She had passed him by, believing she would never be able to rehabilitate such a debilitated horse.

And now he was hers. "I went, oh my God, I got the giant chestnut with the swollen legs, and I am going to have to euthanize him." Conrad was devastated, and terrified. She was not prepared for a horse in such bad shape, or as frantic and distraught as this one. He showed his distress by pawing and trying to rear.

The seller gave Conrad the horse's papers, which listed his name as Clever Ma, and told her he had purchased the horse six months earlier at the same auction. He had intended to fatten him up and get more money from someone who would buy the horse for slaughter. Conrad apprehensively loaded her new horse onto the trailer, and he continued to paw and act anxious the whole way back to the Maryland boarding barn where Conrad would keep him.

When they arrived, she took another look at her new gelding. He was covered with a gluey mud, a probable result of not having been groomed for months. After seeing his legs, which looked like "tree trunks" because they were so swollen, Conrad believed the horse would never be sound. But she decided to watch his movement anyway and turned him out. As she watched him trot she realized not only was the horse an excellent mover but even on those swollen legs, he was entirely sound. Conrad realized she might not have to put this one down after all.

Clever Ma didn't want anything to do with people for his first couple of days in his new home. Then, however, he changed his mind about Conrad. "He kind of stuck his nose in my jacket and stood there, and just kind of took this big sigh, and I think he just knew, OK, I'm safe. I like you." Based upon the condition of his manure, Conrad suspected that the horse had been fed grass clippings. She put him on a special diet to gain weight and gave him six months off to rest, recuperate, and get back to the business of being a horse.

As Conrad and her new horse grew close, she decided he needed a new name. She called him Phinny, as a nickname for Phoenix, which suited perfectly a big red horse that she hoped would rise from the ashes of neglect.

While Phinny recovered from his months of ill use, Conrad began to investigate her new horse's past. She called the people who originally owned the horse, although she was frightened to make a call that could be construed as confrontational, considering the horse's poor condition. That was not the case with Phinny's former owners, the Koskis of Clearview Farm in West Virginia. Instead, they were shocked to hear what had happened to their Clever Ma, who had been born on their farm. The Koskis had held him in their laps when he was a foal, and owned him his entire racing career. They were relieved to hear that he was in good hands.

Conrad also found out her new horse had made a real name for himself as a bad actor at Charles Town Races in West Virginia. "He was a rank horse on the racetrack," says Conrad. In fact, Charles Town people who meet Conrad now can't believe she rides the horse they call "that monster." Yet she trusts him implicitly. "I put my mom on that monster," she tells anyone who doubts his current temperament.

Even though he was ill-behaved at the racetrack, at one point in his life Thoroughbred racing competition was all Phinny knew. His sire is Melodisk, a son of Alydar, and his dam is Asma, by Stoic. Phinny's racing career was solid and workmanlike. He ran from the time he was two until he was six, primarily at Charles Town, although he ran at other tracks as well, including Timonium, Laurel, and Penn National. From fifty-eight starts, he won nine races, and placed or showed in nineteen others. His lifetime earnings were $34,617. His race charts tell a story of many workaday Thoroughbreds. Most races were claiming races, and the comments ranged from "well placed, driving," to "rallied, second best," to "off slowly, no threat."

As the years went by, racing took its toll on Phinny's joints. He had surgery on one knee, and his hocks grew arthritic with age. The Koskis retired their Clever Ma and gave him to someone at the racetrack who they believed was finding good homes for the racehorses. But the horse wound up, instead, at New Holland. The Koskis had given Phinny's full brother to the same person and discovered that horse had not been as fortunate. He had been run through the sale and was gone for good.

Luckily for Phinny, he wound up safe in Conrad's care. After his

Phinny benefited from Allie Conrad's patient handling.

recuperation, Conrad took her horse on the trails and began teaching him to jump. She believes that Thoroughbreds who come off the track learn jumping best outside of the ring over natural obstacles, following an experienced buddy in a low-key, noncompetitive environment. The quiet, steady work paid off, and with his outdoor jumping training, Phinny grew into a natural foxhunter. Once, he and Conrad went out foxhunting on a rainy day, and the rider in front of them got hung up on a coop. Phinny took one nimble step to the left and avoided what could have been a messy accident by hopping the adjacent five-foot fence.

Phinny's care over jumps translated well to the jumper ring and then to horse trials where he placed as high as third in beginner novice and novice competitions. Conrad counts her proudest moment with Phinny as riding her first cross-country course with him in a horse trial at the Carolina Horse Park in 2007. Entering symbolized her faith in all the training Conrad had done with Phinny since she had rescued him from the auction. "The feeling was amazing, even at a low height. He was so proud of himself," she says.

Although she enjoyed showing with her partner, Conrad retired Phinny from competition later in 2008 when he began to struggle to stay sound under a show schedule. Instead of showing, they now work in the ring at his boarding barn or go on long hacks. But retirement from competition has not changed his racer's personality. He does not like to stand still, and Conrad categorizes him as a "hot horse."

Conrad's partnership with Phinny and his journey from neglected auction fodder to beloved companion have fueled Conrad's devotion to the ex-racehorse far beyond caring for her own horse. As the volunteer director of CANTER Mid-Atlantic, Conrad strives to give other ex-racers the opportunity to find caring owners. Her own riding past, culminating in her relationship with Phinny, has led her to dedicate almost all of her spare time to her chosen cause.

Riding seriously since the age of fourteen, Conrad leased her first horse at fifteen. She bought a mare when she was sixteen, and kept that horse throughout her college years. Once her college mount had to be retired, Conrad's veterinarian gave her one of his "racetrack rejects," telling her to be careful, because the horse was "a little kooky."

The horse, whom Conrad calls "a basket case," threw her plenty of times and required a lot of attention. Conrad, who works as a software and Web development specialist, owned that first difficult former racehorse right around the time that online communities sprang up on the Internet. She enlisted over-the-computer help from other people who were involved in retraining off-the-track Thoroughbreds. With the help of others in the same situation, she ended up turning that first Thoroughbred around so significantly that she became intrigued with training ex-racehorses in general. In fact, it was online that she first heard of the horses at New Holland, and came to find Phinny.

She had other forms of help pointing her toward founding CANTER as well. The Koskis, Phinny's breeders, took Conrad under their wing, and along with Conrad have taken up the Thoroughbred retraining cause. The sentiment between Conrad and the Koskis is mutual. "They don't have children, so I'm like their grandkid," Conrad says. She visits them frequently, and they send boxes of carrots and mints to Conrad for the horses in her care.

Getting to know the Koskis cemented Conrad's plan to help other racehorses like Phinny. "I realized that people had no options. Even when they wanted to do the right thing, they had no outlet for these horses. CANTER Michigan had started two years before and I had followed their progress online, and I decided we needed one down here," she says.

Conrad has remodeled her life to fit her mission of finding good homes for ex-racehorses. She goes to her office job at seven o'clock, leaves at four o'clock, and then spends time with Phinny, or checks in on CANTER Mid-Atlantic horses boarded at other Maryland farms. On the weekends she heads to horse shows, giving ex-racers mileage in the show ring, or she goes to the track to evaluate and pick up more horses.

CANTER Mid-Atlantic currently focuses on horses that have raced or been stabled at local tracks, including Laurel, Pimlico, and Bowie, although Conrad is trying to start a chapter at Delaware Park. CANTER Mid-Atlantic's costs run about $60,000 a year, and the organization is funded through private donations, small grants, and the adoption fees of donated horses.

CANTER links horses with people in two ways. For one, owners can donate their horses to the organization. Currently, the organization has twenty to twenty-five horses, and Conrad finds that she has to turn horses away. If the horse comes directly from the track, she and other volunteers take a conformation picture of the horse and all the information that people need to know and put it on the Web site for the public to be able to evaluate. On average, CANTER Mid-Atlantic places twenty horses a year through its retraining program, and 250 a year directly from the racetrack.

Conrad appreciates the difficulty that an unwanted horse can cause. "Even the really good people who want to do right by their horses — if they have a horse that the owner does not want anymore — it becomes an emergency situation. Trainers cannot foot that bill. We try to help them out of that situation." CANTER has helped over 3,000 horses that way.

Conrad says that she finds CANTER owners are an even mix of people who are looking for a pleasure horse that they can just go for walks on, or people who are looking for a competition horse that is inexpensive but has talent that they can bring along. She and her volunteers try to steer people away from having a Thoroughbred as a first horse, but have, on occasion, adopted them out to people who have no horse experience.

Phinny found the right person eight years ago at the New Holland auction. But his purchase has reached far beyond his own experience to help others like him. Conrad classifies her horse as her "priority" and "the absolute pride of my existence." She keeps Phinny sound with very careful management but admits he would probably never pass a vetting, because of all the "lumps and bumps" on him. "You would never imagine that he would be sound. But he just has heart," says Conrad.

The joy of owning Phinny enables Conrad to keep up with her volunteer work, which involves seeing so many horses that are down on their luck or that have to be euthanized because of extensive injury. Being involved with CANTER can be emotionally stressful because some ex-racers don't make it to forever homes because of injury or illness. Phinny helps her feel better about the difficult nature of her position with CANTER, because, as she says, "I'm so connected with him." She hopes to buy a farm of her own in the future, but for now Phinny is kept safe and happy on the grassy hillsides of his Maryland boarding farm.

"This horse is very, very attached to me," she says. "If he hears my car, he comes running. If he hears my voice, he screams and comes running. He has his attention on me all the time. He's almost obnoxious, but any horse that went through the kill pen twice, he can be a little spoiled."

Conrad lets others see the happy product of her hard work with Phinny. Each year she takes CANTER horses to the Maryland Million, a day of fall races at Pimlico featuring state-bred and state-sired horses. During the big day, which includes fair events as well as the races, Phinny, now fourteen, and other CANTER horses parade before a crowd of about 5,000 to raise awareness of the organization. Phinny performs wonderfully at the track, showing off in front of cheering thousands.

Conrad's affection for her big red horse that has made the trip from New Holland to the Maryland Million is obvious. "Everything I have asked him to do, he does. He just will do anything I want. I know he knows he was saved. People just recognize that he's just kind of magic."

Phinny, Conrad says, "is a life force unto himself."

Race and (Stakes) Record						
YEAR	AGE	STS	1ST	2ND	3RD	EARNED
1995	at 2	5	1 (0)	0 (0)	1 (0)	$4,275
1996	at 3	16	4 (0)	1 (0)	3 (0)	$11,078
1997	at 4	21	1 (0)	3 (0)	4 (0)	$7,094
1998	at 5	8	2 (0)	1 (0)	3 (0)	$5,984
1999	at 6	8	1 (0)	1 (0)	2 (0)	$6,186
Lifetime		58	9 (0)	6 (0)	13 (0)	$34,617

Riverdee

By Sean Clancy

13

Over the crackling intercom that interrupted class far too often, I was called to the office — again. As a senior at Unionville High School, I got called to the office my fair share. I either got caught skipping science class with my friend Dave Walton or was failing algebra II, which I had to make up at summer school.

But this time, I didn't know why my presence was being requested up front.

"Your dad's here to pick you up."

Now? Either he had finally found out about algebra II or someone had died.

"I got you something," Dad said as I climbed into his Chevrolet station wagon and we headed down Route 1 South from the sleepy horse country of Unionville, Pennsylvania.

Dad drove with his knee, cracking peanuts and dropping shells on the floor. I did the same, with the exception of using my knee to steer the car. He avoided any hints at what he had gotten me as we made a left on the winding Route 896, which goes from the southeastern corner of Pennsylvania to the northeastern tip of Maryland.

But I knew.

My dad was always buying, selling, trading, and bartering horses. It's the Irish in him. "Dad, we can meet the president of the United States, or we can go to Penn National and look at a horse that might be for sale; cheap horse, probably not worth the gas money to go see him."

Not even a choice.

"Let's go see that horse."

(As I'm writing this, twenty years later, I just called him about a 17-hand Malibu Moon colt. He bought it sight unseen from trainer Rick Violette. That's Dad.)

We made a left onto the gravel driveway of Fair Hill Training Center, back when it was the mere vision of the utopian training center that it is today. Dad trained for George Strawbridge Jr., one of the first owners to invest in the fledgling training center, and the horses were barely worth the stall rent.

We pushed open the creaky, wooden barn door and stepped into the quiet shed row. Gogong, the big gray jumper who had once beaten the four-time champion Flatterer, stopped eating hay and looked at us; the rest of the horses noticed but didn't care. We could see the dust at the end of the barn — like a sideways twister billowing out of the door. And you could hear the commotion coming from the stall, like an assembly line on tilt.

Dad walked down the shed row, suddenly not as excited about what he had gotten me. At the end of the barn, in the last stall on the left, there he was. A little bay gelding, big wide eye popping out of his head, and weaving. More than weaving, it looked like his feet were on fire, as he rocked back and forth from one to the other, shredding his straw bedding like a combine.

Dad looked at him, part disgust, part resignation, part bewilderment. The check had already been written.

"His name's Riverdee."

We slid the metal stall door and stepped into what was left of his bedding. He slowed his weave for a moment, like a jaywalker pausing between cars. He went back to weaving.

Like a practical joke — on his halter it read, "Cage Rattler."

The name stuck. Cage.

A three-year-old bust of a flat horse with one win from twenty starts, beaten twenty lengths for claiming $5,000 in his first and last start for my dad's friend Bobby Connors. He wasn't cooled out before Mr. Connors had called Dad and told him to come see this horse.

Cheap.

Bred by Joseph Shields and Leverett Miller, he wasn't supposed to be this much of a bust on the flat. By Royal and Regal out of a Swaps mare, Royal Swap. He started out with Mickey Preger in New York and couldn't come within a furlong of the winner. He was hammered nine straight times in New York; eighth, twelfth, eleventh, sixth, eighth, ninth, tenth, eighth, ninth, all in maiden claimers. The closest he ever came to the winner was 15¾ lengths in his debut in October 1986. It was also the shortest price he went off, 9-1. Switched to the mid-Atlantic region for trainer Steve Jordan, the Florida-bred began to show a glimmer of life when trying the turf. He finished second in a maiden at Delaware, when it was the bottom of the barrel, then won a maiden over the Atlantic City turf. His form tailed off again and he moved to Connors' barn, where he failed for $5,000 at Philadelphia Park on November 19, 1987.

Dad liked him at first sight when he saw him in the stall. Yes, he was weaving, just staring into the wooden wall, like a prisoner, back and forth, wilting. Dad didn't like his weaving, but he loved his trot.

"There isn't a horse on the grounds who can trot like this," Dad said to himself.

Cage trotted down the grass of the old turf course at Delaware Park. Something they used to call Death Valley, because the stewards couldn't see what went on down in the valley. It was his trot; he flicked his feet Rockette-like fashion, each one delicately placed like he was practicing for a game of hopscotch. Dad knew he could do something with him. That's how he judges horses. For $3,000, he'll make something; steeplechase, eventer, show horse, foxhunter … something … anything.

"You like him?" Dad asked.

"Yeah, he looks nice," I said, with a teenager's distrust. "Does he ever stop weaving?"

"Not sure."

He never stopped. When you buy horses, they don't come with instructions, nor do they come with personality evaluations. It's buyer beware, all the time.

We worked around his weaving. And he worked around us.

For twenty years.

We shipped Cage to Augustin Stable's farm in Pennsylvania, where my father had his second string, thinking he might like the solitude of farm life better than the action at Fair Hill. Wishful thinking. He weaved there, too.

The good news was he could jump. Like nothing I had ever jumped. We did more with him in a shorter amount of time than any other horse I ever remember schooling for my father. Dad played everything conservatively, preaching less is more, son, less is more. With Cage, we just kept asking him questions. Dad put him in the schooling corral and he jumped around there like a gazelle. Dad put me up a few days later and we schooled over logs; just walking and then trotting a stride or two. He did it like he had done it before. I kept asking Dad, "Has he been schooled before?"

Then we jumped bigger logs, no problem. I followed Dad on Student Dancer, a veteran horse who had jumped thousands of fences and was trusted to give any green horse a confident lead. Dad galloped out of the woods and made a right turn, looked back at me I knew where he was going and he knew I knew. Go. Dad and Student Dancer jumped the biggest fence in the woods, a pile of stacked rails, uphill, and Cage followed. Flew over it, jumping like he had jumped his whole life, not for less than a week. We had never jumped a green horse over a fence like that. That's how he did everything.

We introduced him to his first steeplechase hurdle during a blizzard. It had snowed a foot and continued to snow; a powdery snow you could ride through, and again Dad led and I followed. He aimed at the big, imposing National Fence that sat in the middle of the schooling field, the same model they raced over. You could see the top of the black brush, and parts of the green roll; otherwise, it looked like a snowdrift. No problem. He made me feel like I could ride. At least when he jumped.

Jumping, I could hold him. Galloping, now that was a different story. He ran off with me most days. At the time, I thought I could ride him, and it killed me when I realized I couldn't. My father and I owned him. I should be able to ride the horse I own. Not a chance. He wasn't crazy; he just went crazy when speed played into his mind.

We ran him in three flat races at the point-to-points, where they don't offer purse money and the races don't count on a horse's record. Kind of like Triple A baseball. He ran well each time, especially if you consider the eighteen-year-old amateur making the decisions. I did a lot of, 'Should I go here? Should I go there? Should I …' "

He made his steeplechase debut at Radnor Hunt Races in May 1988. He resorted to his morning actions, running off with me in deep ground. He wound up third, miraculously. Only years later did it occur to me how out of control it was for me, hopelessly green, and him, audaciously confident but just as green. We survived, but we knew we had to come up with a better way. He couldn't run off with me and win. Forget winning; he couldn't do it if we expected to survive.

We began to cover him up; I'd break off a touch slow and get him behind horses. He would drop the bit and chill in the back. He made racing easy. He finished third at Monmouth Park in his next start, then finished a good second at the Saratoga Open House, a one-day jump meet before the Saratoga flat meet, despite me trying to sneak up on champion jockey Jeff Teter's inside and bouncing Cage off three beacons on the turn. We ran him back at Atlantic City and he was third again, then we took him to Middleburg where I made the worst mistake of my young career. I forgot to cover him up, just simply forgot, and broke with the field. In a stride, I knew I was in deep water. He ran off, opened up twenty lengths on the field, and I hung on like a streamer, wondering what could be worse, this ride or Dad's reaction. He finished a tiring fourth and I was ashamed of my ride. It was a long car trip home.

Finally, in his sixth start over fences, in a maiden claimer at Red Bank, I did it right and he won. My second career jump win and one of the first times I ever felt like I had accomplished something. Cage was game, snuck past two horses on the outside wing as they

The author and Riverdee at Charleston Races in 1988.

came over on him at the last fence, and sprinted home. After all the holding, all the weaving, all the bollicking from my dad, it was finally worth it.

We ran him twice more, finishing second at Montpelier, with another bad ride from me, and then he finished off the year with a polished performance, winning a decent allowance race at the Charleston race meet in South Carolina.

In all, he made eight starts over hurdles, winning twice, finishing second twice, third three times, and fourth once, (the day I forgot what we had learned) and made more than $20,000. A lot of money for a father and son trying to make it as horsemen. But after Charleston, his left front tendon filled up. Every time you ran your hand down his tendon, the spot gnawed at your gut. It looked bad. We finally scanned his left tendon, and it showed he had bowed. Yup, the little horse — he was 15.3 hands — who always overachieved had broken down. We were overzealous, ran him too much, and paid the price.

We split his tendon, a procedure that had grown popular, and gave him a year off. We brought him back and managed a couple of months of training but his leg wasn't going to hold up to training. It filled up, had heat in it, and made my dad nervous. We didn't want to wreck him, so we looked for an out. He could have made it back to the races, but we couldn't do it to him. The way he weaved, the way he ran off when galloping, and the way he tried in his races, we just couldn't put him through it.

Enter girl.

I was dating Annie Kontos, an event rider in Upperville, Virginia, and I told her about this horse I owned.

"He's a great jumper, an extravagant mover, flicks his feet out, really, really cool."

"What's wrong with him?"

"Well, he weaves, he runs off, and he's got a bow. But you'll like him."

She came to see him at the farm and I cantered to a small hurdle he had jumped at least 100 times, just for her to see him jump. He stopped. He had never stopped at anything, even all those crazy jumps my dad took me over he never stopped. This day, he stopped. I was mortified. She laughed. She liked that for a hurdle horse he still had a spook in him, showed that he was thinking.

She took him on a deal. If you want him, keep him. If you sell him, send us some money. If you hate him, send him back.

She showed him to a couple of prospective buyers, wanted $10,000. He's too small. Ugh, a bow. Too good a mover (never heard that one before). The defining moment came when he popped a bad splint and needed time. Annie asked us what we wanted to do and we made the executive decision to give him to her. He was now an event prospect.

She began his reclamation. In a quieter environment, he began to settle into her program. She had better, more experienced horses at the time and he became the third wheel. Everywhere they went, he went. Horse shows, cross-country schools, events. Bring the mascot.

On a cross-country school with Olympic silver medalist Jimmy Wofford, Annie schooled her first two horses — what she thought were her two best horses — then brought out the mascot and he jumped like he always jumped, simply, easy, no-fuss.

"Who is this horse?" Wofford asked.

"Just a little racehorse Sean gave me."

"You know this is your best horse," Wofford said.

It was the first time anybody praised him, outside the racing world.

Inspired, Cage and Annie set out on a long, educational experience together. He would still run off, still weave, but Annie has a rocklike conviction and wouldn't give in to any of his deficiencies. She bored him when he needed to be bored. She challenged him when he needed to be challenged.

"He'll never fall," I told her, before she started competing him.

If you can hang on, that is.

Tenth at his first three-day, at Bromont in Quebec in spring 1994, Cage returned to Radnor racecourse that fall for its annual three-day event. The same Radnor where he ran off with me in his hurdle debut. He had a flashback. The steeplechase phase was held over part of the old hurdle course, over the same National Fences he ran over. He jumped five hurdles, turned for home with another loop to go, and bolted, leaving out two (maybe three) strides at the hurdle near the finish line. He left the ground so far out, he tried to put down and go again. He didn't fall, but Annie did and their faces met on the ground. I stuck to the story that he wouldn't — and didn't — fall and told her she should have just slipped her reins. Allowing the reins to slide through your hands when a horse's head goes down to the ground is an ingrained survival skill for a jump jockey. After that, Annie switched to a pelham bit for the steeplechase phase.

Annie and Cage eventually came to an understanding; she learned that pulling didn't work, so on a cross-country round, she had to

Annie and Riverdee negotiate a cross-country obstacle.

sit there like she was in a phone booth, sit and wait it out, while he clicked into neverland where he would flat out go. Right about the time when Annie would think, 'I've got to take a pull and slow him down,' he seemed to be thinking, 'This girl is crazy; she's going to kill me,' and then he'd slow himself down.

They never did it better than when he was second at the intermediate level at Fair Hill Horse Trials in spring 1995, through rain, wind, and mud. It was something to behold. Flat out for the first part, then as precise as a code breaker for the latter part. For all of us who knew him, it was special to see him get so good at something that took such discipline.

In the fall, they were in front after dressage and show jumping at the Middleburg Horse Trials. With two jumps to go on the cross-country, I stood on the hillside, in awe as they turned for home thinking the worst was over, we're home free. Then they made a mistake. At the last major question, a corner filled with brush, he misread the question and in midair turned left and jumped through the brush. I swear he was thinking it was a hurdle. On the landing side, he cheated part of another fence that wasn't visible to him, hurtling himself and Annie to the ground. Cage somehow got up; Annie didn't. I ran after him, then ran after Annie. She separated her shoulder, needed surgery. He didn't know what had happened — remember, he had never fallen — but was fine.

The next spring Annie's shoulder still needed time, and she thought it would be prudent for Cage to get some mileage at the advanced level. Olympian Karen O'Connor took the ride on him. They flew around the course in the advanced division at Rolex Kentucky like they were late for lunch, Cage bouncing one strides and in control. They hit the ribbons, finishing eighth in the horse trial division at Rolex in 1996.

After Rolex he went to the intermediate two-star at Essex, but he began to tie up in the vet box after cross-country. He show jumped the next day and finished twelfth.

At twelve years old, the three-day events seemed to be getting tough for him. He meant too much for any of us to risk injuring, or losing. He had become part of our extended family. Annie and I had switched into some kind of "see other people" part of our relationship, but we still had this connection over the horse.

By now, as he was getting older, our Olympic (pipe) dream was over. Annie moved to New York City to go back to school and decided to try show jumping, a city sport. Like always, Cage would adapt. He competed in the amateur-owner jumper division on the A circuit, handling four-foot, three-inch fences with his usual ease. He spent life in the Hamptons and even won a class at the Ox Ridge Horse Show with Annie's trainer, Olympic gold medalist Joe Fargis. Cage lived better than most of us. Eventually he retired from show jumping and came home. Yup, I took him back at age thirteen, and he began his fifth career as a foxhunter with the Cheshire Hunt in my hometown, Unionville.

He was still the same Cage. Great jumper, enthusiastic like a seven-year-old at Halloween and strong whenever the hounds started running. By this time, I knew to sit and wait it out, don't pull, don't panic, he'll never fall. Dad hunted him for a season, I hunted him for about two seasons, and life started taking its toll on him. All heart and less scope than in his younger days, he needed an extra twist to get over the big fences, I could feel his belly scrape over the top rail of the Pennsylvania Hunt Cup fence we jumped at the end of an epic day of hunting. One of the greatest jumps I'll ever feel.

We turned him out for good, about six years ago. His former owners, Joseph Shields and Leverett Miller, and his former trainer Steve Jordan still ask about him when we meet at Saratoga every summer. Today, he's turned out all day, all night, spring, summer, fall, winter, in the front field with a couple of foxhunters and a couple of retirees at Buddy and Kate Martin's farm in West Grove, Pennsylvania, where my father works as farm manager. Cage still has that trot. And that eye. And when he comes in to get his feet trimmed, once a month, he still weaves.

As for Annie, I married her in 2006. We're thinking our first child, Miles, born December 10, 2008, might get his start on an old horse named Cage who lives in the front field. When the baby's three, Cage will be twenty-seven ... is that a sixth career?

			Race and (Stakes) Record			
YEAR	AGE	STS	1ST	2ND	3RD	EARNED
1986	at 2	3	0 (0)	0 (0)	0 (0)	$0
1987	at 3	17	1 (0)	1 (0)	1 (0)	$6,926
1988	at 4	9	2 (0)	3 (0)	3 (0)	$20,320
Lifetime		**29**	**3 (0)**	**4 (0)**	**4 (0)**	**$27,246**

SAMSON

By Virginia Preston

14

The racehorse owner covets a horse with speed, desire, stamina, and pedigree. The mounted police officer envisions a horse with a rare combination of sense, intelligence, work ethic, endurance, and majestic appearance. The dreamer of all things equine imagines this collectively in one horse, and, across the ages, the Thoroughbred has proven to be just that horse. This is the story of one of those horses that embodied the ideal.

Never Round (Never Tabled out of Olympic Breeze) began life in California in 1989, bred for a career on the racetrack but destined for only limited success. After five years so employed, he had amassed $202,080 in earnings, worth a footnote but not spectacular in the annals of racing. Even though he was a stakes winner, his status as a gelding precluded use in the breeding shed. The time had come for a career change. His lineage traced to the illustrious Round Table — a great heritage for a horse who would move into a career of preserving justice.

Barbara Hunter, a Thoroughbred owner/breeder in Nicholasville, Kentucky, donated him to the Lexington (Kentucky) Mounted

Police in 1997. Never Round had been left to Mrs. Hunter by noted southern California Thoroughbred breeder/owner Frances B. Jelks upon her death in early 1996. Mrs. Hunter used Never Round as a teaser — a horse whose job is to detect when mares are in heat and ready to go to the breeding shed. He ran with a band of brood-mares for almost two years until Mrs. Hunter found a potential useful spot for him with the Lexington Mounted Police.

The unit had begun service in 1982 with one officer and horse to meet the city's request for a law enforcement presence at construction sites. By the end of that first year, there were five officers and horses. The horses were trailered eight miles into downtown Lexington from the Kentucky Horse Park. In 1996 a new facility was

Under officer April McCrickard, Samson excelled at crowd control.

built that included a barn, offices, and an indoor arena on ten acres within the city. Currently, ten horses, eight riding officers, and two administrative officers make up the squad.

Officer Lisa Rakes of the Lexington Mounted Police was the new recruit's first rider and trainer. She remembers her first encounter with him, and recognizing the look of strength and substance of this horse, decided he deserved another name so indicative. From this point forward the sleek, black, athletic creature became known as Samson, after the biblical figure symbolic of strength and virtue.

Samson might have been a reincarnation of a splendid warhorse — proud, stately, and poised for the chase. He was 16.3 hands in height and his chiseled features rivaled the beauty of a bronze statue. A good warhorse is magnificent and striking but essentially bred and prepared for action, which inevitably begins with the chase.

His characteristic Thoroughbred nature in combination with his speed and stamina might be well suited to his new designated vocation as a police mount. His greatest success on the track had come in shorter distances — the quick acceleration that would serve him well in his future profession. The real test of his mettle would come after a retraining regimen in the skilled and steady hands of a generous, patient rider.

Chosen for his imposing stature, propensity for speed, and sensitivity, Samson began his training much like any other police mount. Fate had put him into the perfect situation with experienced riders and trainers who patiently redirected and capitalized on these qualities. Lexington was fortunate to have a group of fine police officers assigned to the mounted unit, many of whom were genuinely committed to honing their horsemanship skills. They understood the commitment and were willing to take instructions and spend the required hours in the saddle and on the ground.

In his previous life Samson had been strictly piloted and sent forward by lithe, light riders interested solely in encouraging speed. For the rest of his life, Samson would have a more involved partner working with him. Samson would learn — or not — to respond to and eventually trust the guidance through both the mind and body of a rider, establishing the ultimate partnership. Time in the actual circumstances of his new direction would tell.

Samson's retraining program began with unmounted ground-work, progressed through mounted sessions in the indoor arena, and then time out on the streets. After Samson had spent two months on duty more arena work ensued, including obstacles and distractions to address the weaknesses discovered while patrolling. Periodic arena work would always be a part of life as a police horse to fine-tune both horse and rider. After only six months Samson was officially a member of the mounted squad. New experiences came with the territory — unpredictable and varied.

Samson came equipped with an inconsistent personality and consequent unpredictable behavior. The initial period of service was a challenge to everyone who sat on his back. According to Helmut Graetz, a well-established classical horseman who supervised much of the training of the officers in mounted exercises, jumping, and a multitude of arena drills (and thrills), the horse was either "on" or "off" — no happy medium. "When he was good, he was very, very good — and when he was bad, he was horrid," Graetz recalled.

He could navigate obstacles with great agility, jump with ease and grace, and tolerate activity with indifference or with equal skillfulness; he could spin out from under a rider at the sight of a moving leaf or freeze in his tracks if the spirit moved him. His value when he was "on," however, surpassed his forays into flights of fancy; otherwise, the story would end right here.

Lexington has its share of big city activity and chaos, quite unlike the relative predictability and regimen of life at the racetrack. The sights, sounds, and smells of days on the tarmac proved daunting to many a horse on trial, Thoroughbred nature notwithstanding. Introducing him to the "street" was the first challenge facing Officer Rakes, one of the most skilled members of any mounted police force in the country. Samson slowly and steadily adapted to

Samson grew accustomed to the streets of downtown Lexington.

traffic, construction chaos, and the general pandemonium inherent in crowd behavior. He learned gradually to walk down the city streets and alleys, stand quietly when the situation commanded, and to enjoy the children touching his belly or even ducking between his legs.

Officer Dave Johnson, one of Samson's early riders, was in his own initial stage of the horse/human enigma and development of riding competence. He remembered how impressed he was with the horse's presence and magnificent appearance. "When I first met Samson," he mused, "I remember thinking that this is what Black Beauty must have looked like. I was warned he was not the first choice in the barn for patrol and that he had caused his share of unplanned dismounts. Since I was a rookie to the mounted squad and in my own learning stage, I was quite intimidated, but that soon turned to wonder. As my experience on the other horses progressed, I set my sights on taking him out on duty.

"When that time came, I can remember how empowering the experience was when sitting on his back. There was an underlying power you learned to trust that would be there when you needed it. To his great credit, however, and no matter how much speed you unleashed to get the job done, Samson did have a tremendous respect for the halt and accommodated you with a brilliant stop when it mattered. He was not the bravest of creatures all the time but was brave when it counted most."

Samson was fondest, we might assume, of the chase: pursuing a perpetrator of injustice fleeing on foot until the unwary subject finally was collared or collapsed in exhaustion. Officer Johnson loves to tell the tale of the "great bicycle race":

Mounted on Samson, Johnson was on patrol with Officer Rakes, who was training a new police horse, Jester. As they approached a dark side street, they heard a woman scream and saw a man dragging her toward an abandoned garage. The two officers split up to try to corner the man, carefully making their way through weeds and debris.

Officer Rakes ordered the man to stop, and startled, he let go of the woman and jumped onto a nearby bicycle. He quickly put distance between himself and the officers, careening across a busy road. Jester was a giant of a horse — a "draft" or work horse/Thoroughbred cross — built more for pulling wagons than for a mounted chase. Samson, on the other hand, was built for the chase. "One slight squeeze was all the encouragement Samson needed and we flew past Jester, handily navigated the stream of traffic, and pulled alongside the bicycle," Johnson said. "The subject made several sharp turns, swerved into our path, and nearly made contact a number of times. Samson held his ground, never wavered, and with extraordinary agility, avoided collision. He kept the bicycle pinned between a six-inch curb and us. He put me right in position to reach down and grab the man by the collar and then used his body to slow, then stop, the bicycle and stand steady while the man fought to get free."

The suspect had nowhere to go when Officer Rakes and Jester arrived to complete the apprehension.

Officer April McCrickard, another officer assigned to patrol on Samson, recalled his composure during both routine street duty — writing parking tickets, traffic control downtown — and crowd control for special events with equal praise and awe. She remembered his stamina and crowd-control abilities, noting he could work

Fourth of July festivals immersed in noise and lively celebration with the same aplomb as finding lost vehicles in the mall parking lots during holiday seasons. In addition, McCrickard and Samson worked crowd control at the Kentucky Derby, participated in Mounted Police Horse competitions, and gave demonstrations.

"Samson had a particular strength when it came to rowdy crowds," she said. "Occasionally, when the more experienced lead horse would freeze and not enter the mass of people, he would take over and slowly and forcefully push his bulk into the chaos. He was definitely not unsettled by a sea of bodies — at least not to the extent that they were intimidated by him. His handsome presence drew compliments wherever we found ourselves. He would tolerate the touch and adoration of children and adults alike. He was a pleasure to ride and an honest, reliable partner on duty."

Samson spent more than a decade in service to the people of Lexington with the local mounted police squad. He was sound and healthy and missed only a month or so on the list of the "injured reserves" during his entire career with the mounted police. In addition to the dedication of his officer/riders and local trainers, he

Race and (Stakes) Record

YEAR	AGE	STS	1ST	2ND	3RD	EARNED
1991	at 2	5	1 (0)	1 (1)	0 (0)	$38,265
1992	at 3	13	3 (2)	1 (1)	3 (2)	$132,600
1993	at 4	5	0 (0)	0 (0)	1 (0)	$4,257
1994	at 5	9	0 (0)	2 (0)	3 (2)	$26,807
1995	at 6	2	0 (0)	0 (0)	0 (0)	$151
Lifetime		**34**	**4 (2)**	**4 (2)**	**7 (4)**	**$202,080**

met his annual "continuing education" requirements through work with visiting members of the Royal Canadian Mounted Police and the London (England) Metropolitan Mounted Police. He completed training and a certification with the Pat Parelli School of Natural Horsemanship. Samson competed respectably and successfully in National Police Horse competitions throughout the country. He carried his partners safely, always finishing in the top half of the group and giving his riders solid experience.

A couple months shy of retirement in the spring of 2008, Samson left this life as a result of a crippling kick from another horse in his paddock. There were moist eyes in the toughest of these caretakers of the city. In the words of his partners in service, he will always be sorely missed. In his nineteen years, this horse was loved — and provided security and delight in service to his people.

For those who lived with and loved Samson and from one who shares the passion, rewards of the horse/human bond, and the gratitude of the gift of their presence in our lives comes a tribute, based on a traditional hunting poem:

Hark old horse.
Please meet me at the gate.
We are on duty soon
And we cannot be late.

Step up old horse.
Carry me on the streets.
Our years together count for much.
Though you are no longer fleet.

Move on old horse.
I know you hear the call.
The city is awake.
The folks are on their way.

Kick on old horse.
My partner and my friend.
Our years together on the force
The best that've ever been.

Leap up old horse.
Take the bit and fly!
I still trust you like a brother.
Even though the time is nigh.

Walk on old horse.
We'll soon be hacking in.
Your nicker rests beside my heart.
Our souls entwine within.

Hark old horse!
The years reveal our fate.
If we should part before we wish.
Please meet me at the gate.

SWAMP LINE

BY JENNIFER MORRISON

15

All his life Swamp Line has been a survivor. The tough, jet-black Thoroughbred shrugged off death as a yearling, a knee operation as a three-year-old, and later a stall accident that ultimately ended his racing career.

Blessed with breakneck speed, Swamp Line was a stakes winner as a juvenile but also carried with him the reputation of a rogue — a reputation that haunted him not only on the track but also in retirement, when he met challenges of another kind.

For more than two years, Swamp Line couldn't find a permanent place to call home. He was shuttled from farm to farm, to a foster home for the LongRun Thoroughbred Retirement Foundation near Toronto, Ontario, and to potential adopters who finally decided they could not, or would not, keep the strong-minded gelding.

It appeared that Swamp Line, battle-scarred from the racetrack but strong and sound, was destined to live in foster care in a paddock at a Thoroughbred retirement group foster home with many much older, crippled ex-racehorses.

That is until a fateful day in 2005 when Swamp Line's fortunes changed forever.

Swamp Line came into the world on March 14, 1998, at Ron Clarkson's Rolling Ridge Farm in the historic little town of Alton, Ontario, some forty miles from Woodbine racetrack.

His dam Opening Line had a long racing career in Florida and in Canada but raced just twice after seventy-one-year-old former jockey Bobby Fisher claimed her for just $9,000.

"She had a bum knee," said Fisher in a *Daily Racing Form* interview in 2000. "She was such a nice mare, and I didn't want to hurt her. I never thought she'd get in foal because she was kind of a 'goosey' mare, but she got in foal first crack."

Opening Line's mate, Swamp King, was a stocky, stakes-winning chestnut son of top Canadian stallion Vice Regent.

It was Fisher's first foray into breeding after operating a small claiming stable for many years. In fact, Fisher, who rode the 1947 Prince of Wales Stakes winner, Burboy, was well known in Ontario for his claiming prowess, scooping up cheap runners and patching them up to win stakes.

But for years leading up to the arrival of Swamp Line into his life, Fisher's luck had waned and the wins had dried up.

Swamp Line gave Fisher a new lease on life.

As the only racehorse owned by Fisher and his wife, Joan, Swamp Line was a treasured part of their little family.

"He looked like a little puppy dog when he was born. He was so cute," said Fisher.

Cute, yes, and definitely rambunctious. Paddock antics often left the youngster bumped, bruised, and scratched at the end of each day. And then tragedy nearly struck during the summer of his yearling season when Swamp Line became ill.

"He had an abscess up in his rectum," Fisher said. "He was at [Guelph University Equine Centre] for about ten days. We almost lost him, but he came through it."

In the spring of 2000, Swamp Line arrived on the Woodbine backstretch and began learning the lessons of a Thoroughbred racehorse.

That was when Fisher and his one-horse team would meet jockey Simon Husbands, the only person who would ever ride the newly gelded two-year-old.

"I had just come back to ride at Woodbine from Jamaica," said Husbands, who previously had been at Woodbine for a stint in the early 1990s. "I remember the day so well. I was hanging around the

Swamp Line passed through many hands before finding owner Lesley Kahan.

track kitchen with nothing to do and this little old man came up to me with a cup of tea in his hand and asked if I was a jockey."

Fisher recognized the surname — Husbands' brother Patrick was a leading jockey at Woodbine — and asked if he wanted to get on his homebred.

On the first morning that Husbands arrived at Fisher's barn, he was told by more than one fellow horseperson that the gelding was too tough and dangerous to ride.

"Other trainers and riders told me the horse was crazy. I took him to the gate to break him out of there and he just bolted with me all around the track," Husbands remembered with a laugh. "He was a rude one; there wasn't anything he wouldn't do — in the shed row he bucked, lunged, and kicked anything. He would pull up at the wire sometimes too. But I wanted to ride him."

On the day of Swamp Line's career debut, Fisher told Husbands, "Today you will ride a winner for me. Don't try to slow him down, just steer him."

At 26-1 in a $40,000 claiming race, Swamp Line broke from the gate as if he had been shot from a cannon, and from there he kept getting farther away from his field.

He won by 8¾ lengths in near track-record time for the 5½ furlongs.

A month later, despite suffering a bout with colic, Swamp Line went to the post for the $107,000 Frost King Stakes at Woodbine as the odds-on favorite in a field of six.

Racing under the lights for the first time, Swamp Line raced greenly but led all the way for a nose win.

"He was definitely the fastest horse I had ever ridden in Canada

— still is," said Husbands. "And I was the only one who rode him — he was smart but he was rude. You had to know him and he had to know you."

Swamp Line began his three-year-old campaign with a near miss in the Achievement Stakes — beaten only a head in the $145,000 sprint — and would later win an allowance race before a knee injury stopped his season.

A chip was removed from Swamp Line's knee, and the Fishers gave the gelding all the time in the world to recover before bringing him back to the track in the spring of 2002.

But Freddy, as the horse was affectionately known, was never the same.

"He was lugging out in his gallops worse than ever. He even flipped over and tossed me and then just stood there and looked at me," said Husbands.

One morning Husbands was trying to get the cranky gelding to work when he took off through the exit gap and headed home with Husbands a helpless passenger.

"When I got back to the barn, I found out that Freddy had flipped over in his stall while tied to the wall before he even went out to train that morning.

"I said to the Fishers, that's it, Freddy doesn't want to do it anymore."

The retirement of Swamp Line devastated the Fishers — within one year of Swamp Line's retiring, Bobby had passed away.

Joan Fisher contacted LongRun Thoroughbred Retirement Foundation, based at Woodbine and asked if the organization could help find a home for Swamp Line.

Swamp Line arrived at one of LongRun's foster farms, owned by Mary Zimmerman of Loretto, Ontario, in April 2003.

The gelding fit in well with the other fostered horses at Zimmerman's farm, and in just five months he was attracting prospective adopters including student Amanda Lenting.

"I liked him right away," said Lenting, who visited Swamp Line several times before taking him and a paddock buddy, Sir Frederick, home to her family's small hobby farm where she kept her Arabian/ Paint cross riding horse.

But it wasn't long before Lenting, eighteen at the time, realized that Swamp Line was a bit too high strung for his new surroundings.

Swamp Line initially was high strung and had difficulty settling in.

"When I tried to work with him on cross-ties in the barn, he would get very anxious and nervous, dancing all over the place — especially when he couldn't see Sir Frederick.

"There were always neighborhood kids coming to see the horses, and he was still just too racy; he never settled. I thought he was just too dangerous to be around."

In January 2004, Swamp Line was sedated and vanned back to Zimmerman's farm.

"I didn't want to do it; I felt terrible," said Lenting.

Zimmerman, who has anywhere from eight to ten horses on her farm (some LongRun horses are too injured ever to be adopted) was happy to have Freddy back.

"To me, he seemed very self-contained, sensible, and smart," said Zimmerman. "Sometimes a horse that is happy in one place won't be happy in another. Oftentimes, I would just walk over to him in the paddock and climb on his back."

For eighteen months Swamp Line watched other ex-racehorses come and go and with each day it appeared he was destined to stay in foster care.

But in June 2005, sixteen-year-old Marissa Zulian, seeking a jumping horse, arrived at Zimmerman's farm with a riding coach.

"They came and looked at him in a very businesslike manner," said Zimmerman. "They checked his movement, his size, and they agreed to take him. I really didn't want him to go."

Just six weeks later Zulian returned Swamp Line.

"They said he was getting too strong while they were jumping him and they needed to put a more severe bridle on him," remembered Zimmerman. "I thought to myself, jumping? Freddy had done nothing for years and they were jumping him already?

"Well, they were discouraged, he was unhappy, so he came back to me again."

It was during this time, August 2005, that Lesley Kahan, horse mad from childhood and an office worker for World Wildlife Federation who regularly donated time and money to donkey and draft horse rescue groups, joined the volunteer team for LongRun.

"Everything was driven by horses," said Kahan, who grew up in Toronto, Ontario. "Every single poster, picture, book in my room was a horse and every garbage can or Kleenex box was covered with horses."

As a LongRun guardian, Kahan's job was to follow up on recently adopted racehorses. "I got my first list from LongRun on some horses to check up on and the first name was Swamp Line."

And when Swamp Line's adopter, Zulian, told Kahan she didn't want the horse anymore and wanted to return him to Zimmerman, Kahan was the one who had to report back to LongRun.

"The LongRun group were pretty upset; this poor horse's long-time owner passed away and he had lived in two different homes plus the foster farm … it was sad."

Kahan had always had an idea that one day she would get her own horse. LongRun's Sheri Van Sickle suggested Swamp Line.

"She was stuffing envelopes in the office one day, and I told her that I felt so sorry for this brilliant horse that got passed around from home to home and that whoever got to adopt him one day would be a very lucky horse owner," said Van Sickle. "I really thought she would be a good mother to him."

Kahan was so compelled by Swamp Line's plight that she went

to visit the gelding at Zimmerman's farm, camera in hand to take some file photos.

"The day I went he was covered in mud; he wasn't all that impressive to me, so I went again. That time I took my lunch and just camped out in the paddock with him to see what he would do."

Curiosity, perhaps a little bit of fate, brought Swamp Line to Kahan in the middle of the paddock that fall day in 2005.

"I thought, this guy deserves a forever home; he has a great personality. And if LongRun was going to trust me — talk about dangling a carrot in front of my face," said Kahan.

At home that night, Kahan and husband, Mark, crunched some numbers on costs of supplies and equipment and Kahan asked her riding instructor, Kaleigh Arbuckle, if she could bring Swamp Line to her Glenwood riding stable.

A date was set. Kahan would adopt Swamp Line on November 1.

"I couldn't sleep the whole night; I was excited and nervous. I thought, what am I doing? I was a novice rider, a newbie, I had taken some summer lessons only a dozen times in the five years since this guy had won his first race."

Zimmerman was also nervous — it was the third time she had loaded him on a van to leave her farm.

"I was heartbroken, really. But I learned how much Lesley loved the animals and how she was around Freddy, I knew she was going to love him."

Swamp Line's transition to yet another paddock full of equine friends and another stall in a new barn was not totally without incident.

Re-named Theo (after the *Lord of the Rings* character, King

Lesley has gained Swamp Line's trust and the pair now succeed in the show ring.

Theoden, "king of horses"), Swamp Line soon became the boss of other horses.

"He was great in the barn. He would follow me around like a puppy dog but he was quite dominant in the paddock.

"In the arena, when me or my coach would ride him, he was quite competitive for a while. When a horse came up on the outside of him, he would want to stay in front."

But the scariest incident occurred just weeks after Swamp Line arrived at Glenwood. "It was on our first day in an outdoor arena," said Kahan. "I saddled him up with Western tack so I could have the horn to hang on to, just in case.

"Suddenly some of the neighbor's ducks and geese made noises and Theo took off like he was coming out of the starting gate. We went around the ring hell bent, and the only thing I could see was just a blur."

Kahan wasn't sure what to make of Theo's outburst and wondered if it was a bad habit he would ever break.

"I thought to myself, 'what business do I have being on a horse like this ... is he going to do this a lot because he is a racehorse?' I was never going to give him up, but I was scared."

Kahan persevered and worked with her horse for two years using lunging and voice training, horse behavior clinics, and hours of riding and lessons.

In the spring of 2008, Kahan and Theo shipped to their first show, a dressage primary class.

"I think he was made for shows," said Kahan. "I braided him, he spent a night in a stall for the first time in two years, he went on a trailer again, and then into a portable stall at this show. He was just brilliant."

And in the ring, Theo's flexion, extended trot, transitions from gaits, and overall presentation won the pair their first ribbons — third-place finishes in two dressage classes.

Today, Theo is a far cry from the wild man he was on the racetrack, thanks to the relationship he has formed with the woman who befriended him.

They compete regularly in small dressage shows, spend several days a week together, and continue to learn about each other.

"I love just fussing with him, grooming him, hanging out with him in the paddock. But I also want to become a more proficient rider, and he is helping me do that."

"This was a leap of faith for me," said Kahan. "Who else would take a horse if they had not ridden them or knew what they were about. But I think we were meant to be together."

Kahan has watched several of Theo's races on a DVD she has at home, and her tack room at her barn is filled with photos and albums. She even brought Joan Fisher out one cold winter day to visit Theo is his new home.

"He's being allowed to live the life — a life of a horse," said Kahan. "He gets to eat grass all day and spend some time with me learning new things. Our life together is good together — he's not going anywhere."

Race and (Stakes) Record

YEAR	AGE	STS	1ST	2ND	3RD	EARNED
2000	at 2	3	2 (1)	0 (0)	0 (0)	$89,782
2001	at 3	6	1 (0)	2 (1)	0 (0)	$74,826
Lifetime		**9**	**3 (1)**	**2 (1)**	**0 (0)**	**$164,608**

TRADER

BY ALEXANDRA LAYOS

16

A soft, warm breeze blows across the courtyard as the bay horse walks serenely alongside his female handler. Saddled and bridled, head aloft and ears pricked forward, he surveys his surroundings with interest. The wind picks up, scattering bits of dust from the ground and billowing the horse's short black mane; he gives one great snort.

Ahead of him looms an immense outdoor ring encircled by a high fence with freshly painted white panels and surrounded by apple trees; the sun is warm, and the sand is white. Three horses and riders circle the oval, warming up at various gaits. The girl takes the reins in one hand and reaches up to pat the horse's neck encouragingly.

"Good boy, Trader," she says with a smile. "Welcome to William Woods."

Trader doesn't know what that is, or how he came to be here. It certainly doesn't look like another racetrack, or the New England Thoroughbred Retirement Center where he'd spent the past ten months.

As he raises his head to the wind and flares his nostrils, all he can think is that this must be a new start.

Trader's story began in 2004 in Paris, Kentucky, back when he wasn't known as Trader at all. He was born at Runnymede Farm, sired by The Deputy, who won the 2000 Santa Anita Derby, and out of Pearl Essence, by Horse of the Year Conquistador Cielo. He was registered as Futures Trader, but his nickname around the barn was Freddie. Fully grown, he stood around 15.2 hands tall. He was bay with a white star and two white hind socks.

In 2005 Freddie was taken to the Fasig-Tipton Kentucky fall yearling sale and sold to Michael Imperio for $1,000, a small sum for a well-bred Thoroughbred.

Freddie was put in training, and in 2007 he began his racing career. However, from the very beginning his heart just wasn't in it. He ran once at Belmont Park in New York, once at Delaware Park in Delaware, and three times at Suffolk Downs in East Boston, Massachusetts. He never won a race, and his total earnings amounted to just $658.

Near the end of his very short racing career, Freddie was owned by Danzig Stables. His owners realized that, unlike most racehorses, (and especially the good ones) Freddie didn't have that deep, fervent, and unquenchable desire to run. It was obvious from his five starts — he would never be Secretariat.

But the bay horse was one of the lucky ones; rather than selling him at an auction or allowing him to succumb to some other unknown fate, his owners decided to retire him to the New England Thoroughbred Retirement Center (NETRC), a program based out of Watchtower Farm in New Hampshire and designed to provide excellent care for retired Thoroughbred racers.

Freddie was loaded onto the trailer right from Suffolk Downs and walked down the same ramp in Deerfield, New Hampshire, on October 13, 2007, to view his new home. Upon exiting the trailer, he was greeted by twenty-five acres of rolling green fields, towering sugar maples of orange, red, and gold, and a sparkling pond. Overlooking it all was a nineteenth-century farmhouse and a twenty-two-stall barn with a big wooden sliding door. Five horses were hanging their heads over their stall doors and watching him with interest.

Freddie was turned out in one of the dazzling green fields. He shared a run-in shed and a large pasture with about twelve other horses. He had a lot of room to roam, graze, and gallop as he pleased.

According to David Sears, NETRC executive director, from the moment he arrived that October day, Freddie preferred humans to horses. He found friends in two girls who volunteered at the farm; they thought he was very cute and gave him extra attention. The girls even began riding him and found him to be a fast learner. Although Freddie enjoyed their company and the company of everyone else at the farm, it wasn't until mid-July that he came face to face with the girl who would change his life.

Marissa Parenti came to Watchtower Farm with no intention of changing anyone's life, except perhaps her own. A college student at William Woods University in Fulton, Missouri, Marissa was on a mission to find herself a fresh, new jumping prospect. She had been referred to Watchtower Farm to look at a horse named Judgemeister, about whom she had heard great things.

However, on her way into the barn to look at Judge and the other prospects, she was stopped by a handsome-looking bay horse cross-tied in the aisle way. She noticed that he had a very kind eye. He was a bit skinny, and she soon learned that he was a recent arrival to the farm, still making the transition from aerodynamic running machine to pleasure-riding horse.

He stood quietly as she looked him over, with a cute look on his face as though he were saying a very casual "Hi!"

The first thing Marissa thought was that he would make a nice hunter prospect. She was told that there was already someone involved with the bay horse, working with him and helping to retrain him, and she was too busy to spend much more time with him that day anyway. But as she continued on her way, he never exactly left her mind.

As it turned out, Marissa ended up purchasing Judge, the horse she had originally come to see. She had been fairly set on Judge

Trader (foreground) unwound from racing at Watchtower Farm.

from the beginning, but there was another factor that influenced her decision.

At the time, Watchtower Farm was a home for horses from two different rescue organizations. The NETRC operated out of the farm, but the farm also hosted or "fostered" horses from the Thoroughbred Retirement Foundation (TRF), a national organization. Marissa really wanted to purchase a horse directly from the NETRC, and so Judge was the perfect candidate. The skinny bay horse, on the other hand, was being fostered by the TRF.

However, after the purchase she ended up keeping Judge at Watchtower Farm, and soon began volunteering her time there, quickly becoming assistant executive director of the NETRC. She also continued to keep an interested eye on the bay horse known as Freddie.

She watched as Freddie was taken to his first horse show in July 2008 — the New Hampshire Hunter Jumper Association Summer Festival at the Silver Oaks Equestrian Center in Hampton Falls.

With only two weeks of training with volunteer Jodie Alger, he placed fourth out of twelve horses in the baby green hunter division. Even more so than by the ribbon he won, Marissa was impressed by his demeanor at the show — he was calm, happy, and he did his job without complaint or incident.

Returning to the farm, however, was a different story.

When he came back from the show, he no longer wanted anything to do with the other horses in his field. It seemed to everyone at Watchtower Farm that he had enjoyed his one-on-one training time and his horse show experience almost too much. He wanted more attention than he had previously received when turned out with his twelve pasture mates.

He became distant from them, just standing at the pasture gate, waiting for someone to come and take him inside. He wanted to be fussed with and doted on constantly. He even became grouchy toward the other horses, and they retaliated by picking on him, an easy feat due to his small size. Before long, he was pretty beat up, with all kinds of bite marks covering his body. Freddie's peaceful retirement was quickly falling apart.

Relief came for Freddie after Marissa got the chance to take him for a ride. She was approaching her sophomore year at college, and upon dismounting, she had a sudden idea. Why not take the horse to William Woods? It would be a very unusual move — retirement centers almost never sent their charges to college programs — but the pair had a lot going for them. After all, Marissa already knew the William Woods equestrian science program, and she knew the horse.

During the ride, Freddie had been very cooperative, responsive, and willing to please. However, both NETRC's David Sears and Marissa had noted that his adaptability was perhaps the most important quality for him to have a successful school horse career. At William Woods he would be ridden by many different students, and his short stay at Watchtower had already shown that he could handle different riders.

Freddie was clearly no longer happy with his pasture mates, and life in Fulton would be more like life at the racetrack; William Woods horses do get daily turnout, but Freddie would have his own stall and spend more time inside with people rather than outside with horses. In Marissa's mind, it was the perfect fit, and she began to work on her plan.

Marissa immediately contacted Diana Pikulski, the executive director of the Thoroughbred Retirement Foundation, which at the time was affiliated with NETRC. She explained the situation and why she felt Freddie would make an excellent addition to the William Woods program. At first Diana was a bit skeptical; the organization had tried sending horses to college equestrian programs in the past and had run into some problems. However, because she knew that Marissa was currently enrolled in the program, she decided to give it a shot.

After speaking with Dr. Linda McClaren, associate professor of equestrian science and hunt seat instructor at William Woods, Diana agreed to the adoption. But the work wasn't over for Marissa quite yet.

She made a video of the horse and sent it to Linda to review. Linda said that she trusted Marissa's judgment and told her simply to "figure out the trucking."

This was a challenge — Deerfield, New Hampshire, to Fulton, Missouri, amounts to a journey of more than a thousand miles, a trailer ride that would normally cost about $1,500. However, Marissa contacted Henry P. Welch Trucking in Goffstown, New Hampshire. The owner, Henry Welch, happened to be the father of a close friend of Marissa's.

Certain school horses at William Woods can be leased out during the summer to temporary homes. Henry was already scheduled to take Marissa's horse, Judge, and two William Woods-owned horses that had spent the summer on the east coast, back to Missouri. He had an extra spot on his trailer, so he agreed to add Freddie to the group and bring him to William Woods for free. Freddie was

Trader, with student Marissa Parent, quickly settled into college life.

loaded onto a trailer once again, this time to make the twenty-one-hour drive to Fulton.

Moving halfway across the country is a big enough adjustment, but Freddie also underwent a name change upon his arrival in Missouri. William Woods already had two horses named Freddie in their program, and a third Freddie would've made things a bit ridiculous. So, reverting to his registered name, Futures Trader, they decided to call him Trader.

Trader arrived on August 14, and Marissa rode him during his first weeks at the school, giving him a familiar face with which to connect. According to Marissa, he made the adjustment well.

He gets turned out for an hour every day and is ridden in a riding class most days as well. According to Marissa, he is learning to bend and use himself correctly. Though he is very green, the willing personality Marissa saw back in New Hampshire has continued, and he picks up new things quickly.

Since his arrival at William Woods, Trader has had a myriad of new experiences; he has jumped courses in the large outdoor ring and in the indoor arena. He has taken trips out to the cross-country course. He is brushed and doted on every day, and it's probably safe to say that he is happy.

Trader's pleasant personality, his youth, and all of his yet-to-be-unearthed talent make him the perfect learning tool for all of the

As a young school horse, Trader is learning new skills.

equestrian science majors who dream of becoming horse trainers. Rather than a finished hunter or jumper, Trader, once a high-spirited racehorse, is a young prospect that the students can actually teach from the beginning ... and he can teach them along the way.

He didn't make it on the racetrack, and he wasn't ready for true retirement. But there is more to life than running fast, and for many retired racehorses other opportunities are waiting. That is Trader's lesson, and one that he will continue to impart, student after student, year after year.

Some horses get a second chance. Trader is a rare one that got a third.

Race and (Stakes) Record						
YEAR	AGE	STS	1ST	2ND	3RD	EARNED
2007	at 3	5	0 (0)	0 (0)	0 (0)	$658
Lifetime		**5**	**0**	**0**	**0**	**$658**

TRULY TRITON

BY TRACY GANTZ

17

Bred to be a racehorse, Truly Triton found his real calling tackling the varied obstacles of a cross-country course. Partnered with Olympian Jil Walton, he once made the long list for the Pan American Eventing Championship, excelling in the demanding three-part sport that requires a horse to perform in cross-country, stadium jumping, and dressage.

An enthusiastic jumper whose speed took him far in the eventing world, Truly Triton never would have successfully segued from racehorse to eventer without the help of a dedicated group of people who gave him the opportunity to come back from a tendon injury and take on a career he loves.

Racehorse owner-breeders John Toffan and the late Trudy McCaffery bred Truly Triton, or Attitude Approved as he was known on the racetrack, in 1992. The Canadian duo developed a successful Southern California racing stable and campaigned such runners as Free House and Mane Minister, who each placed in all three Triple Crown races, and 2002 Santa Anita Derby winner Came Home.

Toffan's successful oil business gave the pair the financial capital to follow their lifelong dream of owning racehorses. McCaffery, who lost a long battle with lung cancer in 2007, especially loved horses, having ridden hunters and jumpers most of her life. She had a soft spot for kids and animals, and launched Kids to the Cup, an organization that encouraged young people's interest in racing and took groups to the Kentucky Derby and the Breeders' Cup.

Toffan bought Triton's dam, Coastal Breeze, at the Fasig-Tipton Kentucky mixed sale for $47,000 in November 1991. A modest winner on the track, Coastal Breeze was carrying Triton at the time of the auction, having been bred to With Approval, the 1989 Canadian Horse of the Year and an earner of nearly $3 million.

After the colt was foaled in Kentucky, where the mare was boarded, on April 22, 1992, Toffan and McCaffery registered him under the racing name Attitude Approved. A striking chestnut with a long white blaze, a right hind white sock, and a tiny ring of white above his left hind hoof, he quickly showed the long, lean, straight legs that would serve him well on the track and over fences.

Like most of the other Toffan and McCaffery horses, Attitude Approved went to the barn of trainer Paco Gonzalez, at Hollywood Park in California.

"He was a nice horse to be around," recalled Gonzalez. "He was quiet. He would get a little bit nervous during his races, but not bad."

McCaffery especially liked to give horses time to grow and develop. Though many racehorses begin their careers at age two, McCaffery and Toffan's runners often received several more months or even a year to mature and learn their job. Thus, Attitude Approved didn't begin racing until the fall of his three-year-old season in 1995.

Attitude Approved's sire, With Approval, won many of his top races on grass, a talent he inherited from his sire, Caro, a French champion who raced on turf. Although Attitude Approved's pedigree suggested he might do his best racing on that surface, maiden turf races were hard to come by so he began his career on dirt, losing his first five races.

"He was an honest horse who tried very hard," Gonzalez said. "He could get a little aggressive in his races, though."

That aggression, which often showed up as nervousness in the starting gate, may have compromised his ability to win. In the second start of his career, he got into a bumping match when the gate opened, and he could only finish fourth.

Before switching him to grass racing, Gonzalez tried him once more on the dirt, in a one-mile maiden race at Santa Anita on March 22, 1996. That turned out to be Attitude Approved's only victory. He ultimately started twelve times — four of those on the turf — finishing second twice and third five times for earnings of $70,890.

The wear and tear of racing proved too much for Attitude Approved's right front leg. Gonzalez babied him along, giving him time off when he felt heat in the horse's tendon. But after Attitude Approved finished third in an allowance race on April 13, 1997, at age five, Gonzalez discovered that the horse had bowed the tendon.

It was a small bow, the kind that might have responded to treatment well enough for Attitude Approved to return eventually to racing. But McCaffery and Toffan never pushed an injured horse. McCaffery preferred to give horses away to good homes or sell them for less than they were worth on the track than to race them with a problem.

"We've got to make sure these horses have good second careers after they're done racing," McCaffery would say regularly.

McCaffery and Toffan owned a lay-up facility in Bradbury, a small horse community just east of Santa Anita. There, they kept horses that were headed back to the racetrack as well as those they expected to go on to new careers. Attitude Approved spent several months recuperating from his bowed tendon at the Bradbury farm.

McCaffery had already placed several of their former racehorses with new owners on her own. She had struck up a friendship with Leigh Gray, a former eventer who worked at the racetrack and who had begun finding homes for ex-racehorses in her spare time. They would bump into each other on the backstretch, and McCaffery and Gray soon realized that they shared a love for horses and the desire to find homes for ex-racehorses.

Working for the Southern California Equine Foundation's hospital on the Santa Anita backstretch at the time, Gray was able to place horses with new owners through her connections in the eventing world. She eventually developed her program into a non-profit foundation, the Thoroughbred Rehab Center.

But in the late 1990s, when Attitude Approved was recovering, Gray was putting people and horses together on a much more informal basis. She admired McCaffery's dedication to her former racehorses.

"Trudy would stop on her horses — she didn't want them running at the bottom claiming level," said Gray. "I placed about fifteen of her horses as everything from trail horses to jumpers and eventers."

Gray knew an intermediate-level eventer, Laurie Canty, who had galloped horses at the track. When McCaffery told Gray about Attitude Approved, Gray thought Canty might be the person for him, especially because she knew Canty's experience gave her the ability to train an ex-racehorse.

McCaffery and her farm staff had spent months working on Attitude Approved's tendon, from resting him to hosing the tendon regularly so it would heal. The horse wanted action, but McCaffery wisely didn't allow him to re-injure himself.

By the time Gray and Canty visited him at the Bradbury farm in 1998, he was ready to work again, the tendon cold and strong. McCaffery turned Attitude Approved out in a round pen so that Canty could see how he moved. He dashed around the pen, a dervish in motion.

Even though Attitude Approved bucked and played more than he stepped through his paces, Canty liked what she saw.

"He had a lot of energy," Canty said. "I could tell he was going to be a great prospect. And he only had a small tear in the right front tendon. It never bothered him."

Canty, then fifty-two, had plenty of experience recognizing the type of racehorses that could successfully transition to other disciplines. In her ten years at the track, she had ridden many talented racehorses, including the champion sprinter Precisionist. She liked Attitude Approved's long stride and thought that he had the athleticism to jump well.

McCaffery and Canty agreed on a deal for Attitude Approved. Canty renamed him Truly Triton, evoking a Greek sea god because of the gelding's dam, Coastal Breeze. She put Triton over his very first jumps, and he enjoyed it from the beginning.

"He was always really avid to do it," Canty said. "It didn't take him any time to learn."

Canty soon had to build bigger jumps than usual for a novice horse just to get Triton to pay attention. He began looking for the jumps, "hunting the fences," as jump riders put it. Canty knew she had something far beyond ordinary.

Because of her experience on the track, Canty researched Triton's pedigree. She discovered that his dam, Coastal Breeze, had also produced Heroisbreezin', a 1990 gelding who earned $158,107 during his racing career. However, $136,972 of that came over jumps. Heroisbreezin' competed in East Coast steeplechase events, at times going up against Eclipse Award champion steeplechasers Lonesome Glory, Correggio, and Flat Top.

"I think Triton could have been a steeplechaser," Canty said, "anything fast on the grass. He never really looked fast. He just got lower to the ground."

While Triton carried his speed well over a jump course, he still had that racehorse mind, revving up and getting overly excited when asked to perform. Canty spent months riding him, learning his quirks, and settling him down. Yet Triton never needed much guidance over jumps.

"When you put his face in front of a fence, he'd do his job and focus," Canty said. "I wouldn't have anything to do."

As Canty continued to work with Triton, she called on Jil Walton for help. Walton specialized in turning novice event horses into top-level competitors. She had ridden for the United States in the 1991 Pan American Championships and the 1992 Barcelona Olympics. In the Olympics she partnered with the mare Patrona, another former racehorse, to finish as the highest-ranking U.S. pair.

Canty had trained off and on with Walton, who aided her in getting Triton to the next level.

"We just clicked," Canty said of her experience riding with Walton. "I would haul horses out there, and she would figure out what we needed."

Canty rode Triton in his first horse trial in March 1998. Walton

Truly Triton's natural jumping ability impressed Jil Walton.

was helping as Canty and Triton's coach and falling in love with the horse.

"I knew she was lusting after him," Canty said, laughing at the memory.

Triton had so much energy and ability that Canty eventually and reluctantly realized he needed a younger rider. As Triton progressed into a more accomplished eventer, Canty began receiving offers to buy him. Walton assembled a group of investors and purchased him after Canty had showed Triton for a couple of years.

Though many eventers prefer Warmbloods, Walton liked Thoroughbreds because of how fast their minds work. That was one of the traits that drew her to Triton. She also loved his athletic ability and recognized his jumping potential.

"He was one of those horses who had a sense of where his whole body was," Walton said. "He could jump anything."

Having worked with Canty and Triton for so long, Walton was able to move forward in the horse's event training without missing a beat.

As Triton progressed up the levels with Walton, the cross-country courses became more difficult, but his natural jumping ability allowed him to succeed without always paying full attention to his work. Ironically, it took a fall to launch him to the upper levels of the eventing world.

Heading over an oxer while competing at the cross-country course in Fair Hill, Maryland, in 2001, Triton tried to take the jump too fast. He hooked his left hind foot on the jump and managed to spike a piece of the jump into the hoof.

Walton had to doctor the foot for quite a while, and she said he seemed to know she was helping him. When he went back into training ten weeks later, he found new focus, almost as if he was determined not to hurt himself again.

"He's one who definitely got to me," Walton said. "He had such a sense of himself."

Triton's racehorse speed meant Walton never had to worry about making the required time in either the cross-country or stadium jumping portions of eventing. He was particularly handy in corners on cross-country courses. The gelding followed Walton's direction over jumps, though he could get overconfident with combinations.

Often, Triton would pay close attention going over the first two of a three-fence combination. He would see that only one fence remained and lose focus, dropping his hind feet and either clipping or sometimes knocking down the obstacle.

Triton's speed hindered him in his dressage work.

"He didn't calm down in dressage until he was twelve," Walton said. "The dressage section was always his weak spot. He just didn't have that big, floaty trot."

Under Walton's patient handling, Triton eventually developed his dressage ability to the point where he and Walton were competing at the highest eventing levels in the country.

In 2003 Walton and Triton finished ninth in the Foxhall Cup in Georgia, which Walton thinks was their best performance together, though they won and placed in many other events. Their accomplishments that year earned them a spot on the long list for the 2003 Pan American Eventing Championship at Fair Hill.

They also competed in one of eventing's premier shows, the

2004 Rolex Kentucky Three-Day Event. However, during the cross-country phase, Walton approached a water obstacle too slowly. Triton was supposed to bounce from an obstacle into the water, but instead he tried to put in an extra stride, perhaps distracted by a nearby grandstand of observers.

Walton fell, though she avoided getting wet. She gamely re-mounted Triton, finished the course, and even competed in the stadium jumping. But the penalties accrued in the fall ended any chance for a placing.

One remnant of Triton's racing days gave him a peculiarity in cross-country. Perhaps because he learned to walk to a starting gate accompanied by a pony, he couldn't go to the start box of a course by himself.

Truly Triton and Jil Walton compete at the Rolex-Kentucky Three-Day Event.

"Someone would have to lead us on foot," Walton said.

By 2005 Triton was thirteen years old. Walton was planning an eventual move from California to Montana, and that coupled with his age meant it would soon be time to sell him. She was coaching more riders by then, and one of her students who showed Triton was college student Natalie Stephens of Huntington Beach, California.

Natalie began her riding career on hunters and jumpers but soon switched to eventing. With Walton as her coach, Natalie rode at intermediate-level events, often showing Triton. Natalie's mother, Patty, a pediatrician, also enjoyed riding, though she had never competed in shows. She began taking lessons with Jil on Triton.

"I'm a beginner," Patty said. "But I could see that this horse knew eventing. He was just so well trained. He listened, and he knew his job."

When Triton became available for sale in early 2006, Patty bought him from Walton.

"I told Natalie that this would be great because both of us could ride him," Patty said. "How many horses can do this? This is a great horse for her to learn and move up the ranks on."

As pre-veterinary classes at Scripps College in Claremont, California, began occupying much of Natalie's time, Patty found herself riding Triton more often.

"While she's at school, he's teaching me to jump," said Patty.

The confidence Triton instills in his riders meant even more to Patty, who had broken her neck and her collarbone in a fall from another horse. Not only did Patty have confidence riding Triton because she could see how much he knew and how well he could jump, she learned to trust him even more after she fell off of him.

Schooling in an arena, Patty became distracted by a commotion at the other end of the ring. She glanced over at the other riders while Triton soared over a jump. Because Patty wasn't looking at the jump as she had been taught, she was unbalanced and fell, landing on the fence and breaking her finger.

Triton stopped immediately. Patty still had the reins in her hands, and she realized in horror that Triton could easily have dragged her across the arena. Instead, he knew she was in trouble and took care of her.

Patty plans to take care of him for the rest of his life. He lives on her small acreage in Rancho Carrillo, California, not far from San Juan Capistrano. Natalie may continue to show him occasionally as her studies permit, but it is Patty who will likely be Triton's companion in his later years.

"I feel so thrilled to ride him," Patty said. "The horse has a heart of gold."

Race and (Stakes) Record

YEAR	AGE	STS	1ST	2ND	3RD	EARNED
1995	at 3	3	0 (0)	0 (0)	2 (0)	$13,125
1996	at 4	5	1 (0)	2 (0)	1 (0)	$46,725
1997	at 5	4	0 (0)	0 (0)	2 (0)	$11,040
Lifetime		**12**	**1 (0)**	**2 (0)**	**5 (0)**	**$70,890**

WITH EASE

By Rena Baer

18

With Ease was never meant to be a racehorse. And, for all intents and purposes, he never was. Well, maybe just for all purposes, because the intents were definitely there. Not his, mind you.

His story is one of irony, how small a world it really is, and caring individuals who realized he was never going to make it to the track and sent him off on a different path.

With Ease was born in 1995, in Midway, Kentucky, a small town that is the postcard image of horse country. He was bred by Glencrest Farm, a large, family-run breeding and racing operation started in the 1950s by John Greathouse Sr. and passed along to his four sons — John Jr., Allen, David, and Edward. The farm sits on nearly 1,000 acres of fields and barns shaded by big bur oak, walnut, and blue ash trees. With Ease could not have dropped into a more picturesque equine setting, and he arrived with a good pedigree and a lot expected of him.

He was the product of one of the farm's many broodmares, Empress of Love, a former stakes-placed racehorse, being bred to the well-known Easy Goer for a stud fee of $50,000.

"We bought the mare and raced her in a couple of stakes and she did well," said Allen Greathouse. "Later we bred her to Easy Goer, thinking we had hit a home run."

Easy Goer had yet to be proven as a stallion, but his accolades as a racehorse included being named champion two-year-old and winning the 1989 Belmont Stakes. He also was the son of the famed Alydar, who had segued from stellar racehorse to successful sire until his untimely death in 1990.

On paper the future looked bright for the chestnut colt, but a bad-looking set of ankles and a gangly body that bore no semblance to that of a racehorse complicated the picture. When Glencrest sent its consignment to the 1996 Keeneland September yearling sale, where the farm sells many of its youngsters, the colt did not meet his $10,000 reserve. Instead, he was brought back home to race but showed little inclination to run.

"He just never had the instinct," said Cyndi Greathouse, who is married to Allen Greathouse. "He was more like a puppy dog than a racehorse."

The horse was later sold as a two-year-old in 1997 through a bloodstock agent to Mike Stierstorfer, a Philadelphia dermatologist, and Tim Foster, a Boston orthopedic surgeon. The two men, both racing fans and first-time owners, paid $15,000 for the colt, sight unseen, along with $10,000 for a Dynaformer colt they named Totally Hip, after the total hip replacements that probably helped pay for him. They chose the two from a list of six Thoroughbreds the bloodstock agent told them about, said Stierstorfer. They liked that With Ease was by Easy Goer and decided to take a chance even though they were told he had a bone chip in his ankle.

They put the horses under the tutelage of a college friend's wife, who had initially put them in touch with the bloodstock agent through whom they had purchased the colts. She lived in Kentucky and had just starting training Thoroughbreds. The two horses stayed with her for a year, with Totally Hip running in a couple of races and With Ease reportedly making progress toward that end.

The two doctors eventually decided to move the horses to Delaware Park, where they could watch them run. A bloodstock agent they had met while attending the Travers Stakes at Saratoga Race Course gave them trainer Steve Jordan's name. Jordan, who now works for the New York Racing Association, said he agreed to train the horses after being told one had already been racing and the other, With Ease, had yet to race but was only a few weeks from being ready.

When the horses got off the van at Delaware Park, Jordan said he realized right away that With Ease was far from being ready to race. "His belly was hanging to the ground, he had no shoes, and his hooves were all cracked," Jordan said. "Not to mention, he had ligament injuries."

He immediately called the owners and told them that they needed to cut their losses and get rid of With Ease and that he had just the person to take him, Maryland veterinarian Kathleen Anderson, who sometimes took former racehorses and found homes for them.

Anderson was in the hospital having her second child when Jordan called her about With Ease. He told her how the horse could not hold up to training and he didn't want him to end up in the wrong hands. As soon as the soft-hearted Anderson could, she went to look at him.

"He had four white socks, a white blaze, and only one sound leg on him," she said. "He looked like he needed some time."

Anderson offered the doctors $500 for him, which the two men accepted. Stierstorfer said it wasn't a tough decision, given that they had poured a lot of money into him without having gotten a race out of him, and that they knew he was headed for a good home. Plus, their other horse, Totally Hip, was doing very well and winning races here and there.

For two years Anderson took care of With Ease, renaming him Just John for her first child, John, who when asked as a little boy if he had a last name would tell people "Just John." Anderson let Just John recover in a field, with plenty of space to stretch his legs. The last six months she owned him, she put him under saddle and began working with him.

Megan Carr rode Jonathan to many victories.

"All he needed was some time and Mother Nature to mature," she said. "He was so high strung when he arrived, and by the time he left, you could wave a flag in front of his face."

When Anderson realized she couldn't give him the attention he deserved and the purpose he needed, she decided to find someone who could. While at an American Association of Equine Practitioners convention she ran into a friend of hers, Joe Carr, whose daughter Megan, a high school junior, showed one of Anderson's horses, No Worries. For a few years Megan had been three-day eventing with No Worries, sending him back up to Fair Hill, Maryland, for Anderson to trail ride during the winter. When Anderson asked about No Worries, who was about to head back to Maryland, Carr told her the older horse's feet were starting to go. Anderson asked Carr whether Megan was ready for "a project."

John arrived at the Carr household in Lexington right around Christmas 2000, as a gift, with a big red bow on him. All Megan knew about the horse before he arrived was that he was a five-year-old Thoroughbred gelding. After years of riding and working with bays, she had pictured just that getting off the eighteen-wheel trailer.

"I had never had a chestnut — let alone a strawberry roan chestnut," she said. "He was huge (16.3 hands) and gorgeous. The name John just didn't fit him; he needed a much more magnificent name like Jonathan."

The next morning she was so excited to try him out that she threw a halter on him and rode him up to the barn bareback. He was very calm, she said, but very green. All of the other horses Megan had previously ridden for three-day eventing — which consists of dressage, cross country, and stadium jumping — had been well-schooled and were basically push-button.

"He was the first horse I was able to bring along all the way," she said. "And he turned out to be amazing, though it took him a little while to realize that all four legs worked together."

Once he figured it out, Jonathan became a quick learner. As the two worked with trainers, Jonathan became particular, wanting his rider to give precise direction.

"He taught me a lot," Megan said. "Most of all, if you didn't ask correctly, you weren't going to get it."

The pair quickly began competing and doing well, working their way from novice classes to qualifying for major events when Megan was a freshman at the University of Louisville. That year, though, her parents divorced and her riding plans were derailed as finances and being busy with school became issues. Jonathan was sent to Florida to stay with her aunt for a year.

When he returned to Kentucky, Megan and her father tried to sell him, but his bad-looking ankles turned many prospective buyers away. His X-rays showed degenerative joint disease, but Megan said the horse had never taken a bad step and had passed his flexion tests. She ended up leasing him to a family that she said did not take care of him. When the year-long lease was up, Megan and her father did not renew it.

Without the time or resources to keep him herself, she and her dad began to look for someone else, carefully vetting people.

"I was very apprehensive about leasing him again," Megan said. "If he was going to go to a show, I wanted to know, and I wanted a report on how he did. I wanted to know what his vaccination schedule was."

Joe Carr, a racing fan and horse show judge who worked as a vet tech before selling equine insurance, said his daughter grew so much with Jonathan, learning lessons of love, caring, responsibility, and horsemanship, not to mention the value of money. He said he also became very attached to the horse, going to all their shows and cheering them to victories.

"I wore the same outfit every day that horse ran — a crappy black Polo shirt and a Giant's Causeway hat for good luck," he said.

In 2006, Joe Carr remarried; his wife worked at the Keeneland Pony Club. One day someone came in asking if anyone knew of a horse one of the club's members, Nicholas Greathouse, could lease and show. He was just on the verge of becoming a teenager and had outgrown his pony.

"He was a good horseman, so we thought we'd take a crack at it," Joe Carr said.

Nicholas Greathouse has taken over from Megan with Jonathan.

When they brought Jonathan to the Greathouses, Allen Greathouse took one look at his son's newly acquired show horse and knew exactly who he was. He told Joe Carr, "I remember that horse. He couldn't get out of his own way."

Though Allen Greathouse has seen many horses in his lifetime, he said With Ease stayed with him. "You remember the good ones, and you remember the ones you lost your shirt on."

Nicholas, now fourteen, is still showing Jonathan and doing well with him and winning events, including multiple regional championships in 208; Megan, who graduated college and works in Louisville, is still always checking up on him; and Joe Carr is still there watching every one of his shows and videotaping them.

"He is the worst videographer ever," said Megan. "He is running the whole way around with him, so you can hear him breathing on the tape, and every time Jonathan and Nicholas jump, so do Dad and the camera."

There's no question that this horse is loved.

"We're already arguing about where he'll retire," said Megan.

Kathleen Anderson, who gave Jonathan to Megan, said he's a good example of a racehorse that went through the system and found his calling in a different discipline.

"We need a set way to get them second lives," she said. "Until we have that, we are all part and parcel of the big picture. Everybody should do their part. We need a huge solution, but small solutions are a step in the right direction. Jonathan's story goes to show how many lives we can touch with one horse."

Equine Rescue Resource Guide by State

ALASKA

■ Alaska Equine Rescue
P.O. Box 771174
Eagle River, AK 99577
888-LUV-HORS
www.alaskaequinerescue.homestead.com
Email: aer@alaskaequinerescue.com

CALIFORNIA

■ California Equine Retirement
Foundation (CERF)
34033 Kooden Rd.
Winchester, CA 92596
951-926-4190
www.cerfhorses.org
Email: cerf1@earthlink.net

■ CANTER California
260 Las Miradas Dr.
Los Gatos, CA 95032
www.canterusa.org/california
Email: canterca@canterusa.org

■ Tranquility Farm
20595 Pegasus Rd.
Tehachapi, CA 93581
661-823-0307
www.tranquilityfarmtbs.org
Email: info@tranquilityfarmtbs.org

■ United Pegasus Foundation
120 South First Ave.
Arcadia, CA 91006
626-279-1306
www.unitedpegasus.com
Email: unitedpegasus@yahoo.com

COLORADO

■ Colorado Horse Rescue
10386 N. 65th Street
Longmount, CO 80503
720-494-1414
www.chr.org
Email: info@chr.org

■ Horse Protection League
P.O. Box 741089
Arvada, CO 80006
303-216-0141
www.cohpl.org
Email: info@cohpl.org

CONNECTICUT

■ H.O.R.S.E of Connecticut, Inc.
43 Wilbur Rd.
Washington, CT 06777
860-868-1960
www.horseofct.org
Email: hocinfo@yahoo.com

DELAWARE/MARYLAND

■ CANTER Mid-Atlantic
301-980-0972
www.canterusa.org/midatlantic
Email: allie@canterusa.org

■ Days End Farm Horse Rescue
P.O. Box 309,
Lisbon, MD 21765
301-854-5037
www.defhr.org
Email: info@defhr.org

■ Equine Rescue & Rehabilitation, Inc.
16724 Miller Lane
Parkton, MD 21120
www.horserescue.com
Email: equinerescue_rehab@yahoo.com

■ Horse Lovers United, Inc.
P.O. Box 2744
Salisbury, MD 21802-2744
410-749-3599
www.horseloversunited.com
Email: horse@intercom.net

■ Mid-Atlantic Horse Rescue
284 Great House Farm Lane
Chesapeake City, MD 21915
302-376-7297
www.midatlantichorserescue.org
Email: bev@midatlantichorserescue.org

DISTRICT OF COLUMBIA

■ Unwanted Horse Coalition
1616 H Street, NW, 7th Floor
Washington, DC 20006
202-296-4031
www.unwantedhorsecoalition.org

FLORIDA

■ Horse Protection Association of
Florida, Inc.
20690 NW 130th Ave.
Micanopy, FL 32667
352-466-4366
www.hpaf.org
Email: morgan@hpaf.org

GEORGIA

■ Georgia Equine Rescue League, Ltd.
P.O. Box 787
Locust Grove, GA 30248
404-656-3713 or 800-282-5852
www.gerlltd.org;
Email: info@gerlltd.org

IDAHO

■ Orphan Acres, Inc.
1183 Rothfork Rd.
Viola, ID 83872
208-882-9293
http://personal.palouse.net/orphanacres
Email: orphanacres@hotmail.com

ILLINOIS

■ Hooved Animal Humane Society
10804 McConnell Rd.
Woodstock, IL 60098
815-337-5563
www.hahs.org
Email: info@hahs.org

■ CANTER Illinois
198 Applewood Lane
Bloomingdale, IL 60108
630-341-1582
www.canterusa.org/illinois
Email: canteril@canterusa.org

KENTUCKY

■ Kentucky Equine Humane Center
1713 Catnip Hill Rd.
Nicholasville, KY 40356
859-881-5849
www.kyehc.org
Email: lneagle@kyehc.org

■ Old Friends Equine Sanctuary
1841 Paynes Depot Rd.
Georgetown, KY 40324
502-863-1775
www.oldfriendsequine.org

■ ReRun, Inc.
(also see ReRun New Jersey)

■ Speak Up For Horses
P.O. Box 434
Falmouth, KY 41040
859-445-7766
or 513-474-6626
www.speakupforhorses.org
Email: info@speakupforhorses.org

■ TRF Maker's Mark Secretariat Center
4089 Iron Works Pike
Lexington, KY 40511
859-246-3080
fax 859-246-3082
www.thoroughbredadoption.com
Email: nvoss@trfinc.com

MASSACHUSETTS

■ CANTER New England
P.O. Box 3
Westborough, MA 01581
781-354-6291
www.canterusa.org/newengland
Email: canterne@canterusa.org

■ Kings Bridge Equine Rescue, Inc.
7 Kings Bridge Rd.
Brimfield, MA 01010
413-283-7419
www.equineresq.org
Email: rescue@equineresq.org

■ Suffolk Downs
111 Waldemar Ave.
East Boston, MA 02128
617-567-3900
www.suffolkdowns.com/retirement.html

MICHIGAN

- CANTER Michigan
  2760 East Lansing Drive, Suite 5
  East Lansing, MI 48823
  810-384-8410
  www.canterusa.org/michigan
  Email: cantermichigan@canterusa.org

- Second Career Racehorses
  25 South Division
  Grand Rapids, MI
  616-913-2790
  Email: scr@cybernet-usa.org

MINNESOTA

- Minnesota Hooved Animal Rescue, Inc.
  P.O. Box 47
  Zimmerman, MN 55398
  763-856-3119
  www.mnhoovedanimalrescue.org
  Email: info@mnhoovedanimalrescue.org

- Misfit Acres
  12480 550th Ave. W
  Amboy, MN 56010
  507-278-4876
  www.misfitacres.com
  Email: info@misfitacres.com

NEW JERSEY

- Mylestone Equine Rescue
  227 Still Valley Rd.
  Phillipsburg, NJ 08865
  908-995-9300
  www.mylestone.org
  Email: mer@eclipse.net

- ReRun, Inc.
  P.O. Box 113
  Helmetta, NJ 08828
  732-521-1370
  www.rerun.org
  Email: rerunnj@comcast.net

- Standardbred Retirement Foundation
  108 F Old York Rd.
  Hamilton, NJ 08620
  609-324-1500
  www.adoptahorse.org
  Email: Jennifer@srfmail.com or
  gen@srfmail.com

NEW MEXICO

- The Horse Shelter
  100 AB Old Cash Ranch Rd.
  Cerrillos, NM 87010
  505-471-6179
  www.thehorseshelter.org
  Email: info@thehorseshelter.org

NEW YORK

- Thoroughbred Retirement Foundation
  (TRF)
  P.O. Box 3387
  Saratoga Springs, NY 12866
  518-226-0699
  www.trfinc.org
  (Chapters in numerous states)

- New York Horse Rescue Corp.
  P.O. Box 435
  Manorville, NY 11949
  631-874-9420
  www.nyhr.org
  Email: Mona@nyhr.org

- H.O.R.S.E Rescue & Sanctuary
  P.O. Box 432
  York, NY 14592
  585-584-8210
  www.hrsny.com
  Email: rescue@rochester.rr.com

- ReRun, Inc.
  (also see ReRun New Jersey)
  Email: reruntb@yahoo.com

OHIO

- CANTER Ohio
  3967 Karl Rd. #228
  Columbus, OH 43224
  614-266-3975
  www.canterusa.org/ohio
  Email: canteroh@canterusa.org

- New Vocations
  3293 Wright Rd.
  Laura, OH 45337
  937-947-4020
  www.horseadoption.com
  Email: info@horseadoption.com

PENNSYLVANIA

■ Appalachian Horse Help & Rescue
1201 Yergers Rd.
Linden, PA 17744
570-322-3260
Email: Lae764@hotmail.com

■ Bright Futures Farm
44793 Harrison Rd.
Spartansburg, PA 16434
814-827-8270
www.brightfuturesfarm.org
Email: info@brightfuturesfarm.org

■ CANTER Pennsylvania
55 Sipe Rd.
Carlisle, PA 17013
717-385-0169
www.canterusa.org/pennsylvania
Email: canterpa@canterusa.org

■ Ryerss Farm for Aged Equines
1710 Ridge Rd.
Pottstown, PA 19465
610-469-0533
www.ryerssfarm.org
Email: ryerssfarm@verizon.net

TEXAS

■ Habitat for Horses, Inc.
P.O. Box 213
Hitchcock, TX 77563
866-434-5737
www.habitatforhorses.org
Email: admin@habitatforhorses.org

■ LOPE Texas
1551 Highway 21 West
Cedar Creek, TX 78612
512-565-1824
www.lopetx.org

VIRGINIA

■ Roanoke Valley Horse Rescue, Inc.
P.O. Box 13
1725 Edwardsville Rd.
Hardy, VA 24101
540-797-1999
www.rvhr.com
Email: info@rvhr.com

WASHINGTON

■ Second Chance Ranch
P.O. Box 899
Elma, WA 98541
360-861-8056
www.secondchanceranch.org
Email: info@secondchanceranch.org

ONTARIO

■ LongRun Thoroughbred Retirement
Society
555 Rexdale Blvd.
P.O. Box 156
Toronto, Ontario M9W5L2
www.longrunretirement.com
Email: info@longrunretirement.com

Photo Credits

Chapter 1: Anne M. Eberhardt, 11

Chapter 2: Courtesy Tara Ziegler, 24, 26, 29

Chapter 3: Courtesy Katie Merwick, 34, 39, 42, 43

Chapter 4: Benoit & Associates, 47; Ellen Pons, 49

Chapter 5: Coady Photography, 60; Anne M. Eberhardt, 66, 67

Chapter 6: Courtesy Santa Anita, 74, 76,79, 80; Wendy Hall, 77

Chapter 7: Megan Arszman, 84, 86

Chapter 8: USTA/Ed Keys, 98; Racehorsephoto, 100

Chapter 9: Courtesy Shelly Price, 105, 107

Chapter 10: Courtesy Paula Drake, 119, 123, 124

Chapter 11: Courtesy Jennifer Morrison, 128, 129, 132, 136, 137

Chapter 12: Eliza McGraw, 143

Chapter 13: Catherine French, 155; Courtesy Sean Clancy, 159

Chapter 14: Courtesy Lexington Mounted Police, 164, 167

Chapter 15: Courtesy Lesley Kahan, 175, 178, 182

Chapter 16: David Sears, 188; Tom Baker, William Woods College, 192, 193

Chapter 17: Quince Tree Photography, 201; Shannon Brinkman, 204

Chapter 18: V.W. Perry, 210; GRC Photography, 213

Cover: Rick Samuels (Funny Cide)

About the Authors

Rena Baer is a Lexington, Kentucky, freelance writer and editor who has contributed to several Eclipse Press books and special publications. Her work also has appeared in *Keeneland* magazine, *The Lane Report*, *Small Market Meetings*, *Panache*, and several other publications. In addition, she is a copy writer and editor for Roskelly Inc. of Newport, Rhode Island.

Alexandra Beckstett is assistant editor of Eclipse Press, the book division of Blood-Horse Publications. She has written for the *Chronicle of the Horse* and *Keeneland* magazine and worked as an editor of TIPS Technical Publishing while attending Duke University.

Jennifer Bryant is the editor of *USDF Connection*, the member magazine of the U.S. Dressage Federation. She has written several books, including *Olympic Equestrian: A Century of Equine Horse Sport* and *The USDF Guide to Dressage*. An avid equestrian, Bryant lives in Pennsylvania.

Sean Clancy is an award-winning sports journalist and former champion steeple-chase jockey. He is the author of several books, including *Barbaro: The Horse Who Captured America's Heart*. Clancy is the editor/publisher of ST Publishing, which produces a number of racing publications.

Amanda Duckworth is a staff writer for *The Blood-Horse* magazine. She is a graduate of the University of Kentucky and lives in Lexington.

Tracy Gantz is the Southern California correspondent for *The Blood-Horse* magazine. She is also a regular freelance contributor to the *Paint Horse Journal*, *Performance Horse*, and *Appaloosa Journal*. She began her career at *The Blood-Horse* and also served as the West Coast breeding columnist for *Daily Racing Form*.

Alexandra Layos is completing her undergraduate degrees in both communications and equestrian science at William Woods University in Fulton, Missouri. Along with riding, Layos is an avid reader and a writer. She writes for *Saddle & Bridle* magazine and has written several children's books. Layos' work also has appeared in *Horse Tales for the Soul: Volume 2* and *Of Women and Horses: More Expressions of the Magical Bond*.

Eliza McGraw has contributed to several Eclipse Press collections. Her work has appeared in *The Blood-Horse* magazine, *EQUUS*, and the *Chronicle of the Horse*, among other publications. She lives in Washington, D.C. and rides in Potomac, Maryland.

Katie Merwick is a native of Washington state. An animal behaviorist, Merwick founded Second Chance Ranch, a horse rescue organization devoted to the rehabilitation and adoption of Thoroughbreds. She has been recognized by the American Red Cross with its 2001 Hero of the Year Award, and in 2008 received the Washington Thoroughbred Breeders Association Special Achievement Award for her work with Thoroughbreds at Emerald Downs.

Jennifer Morrison lives in Brampton, Ontario, Canada, and has covered and handicapped horse racing for more than 20 years. She has been the oddsmaker for Woodbine racetrack for more than a decade, writes and handicaps for the Toronto *Star* and *Daily Racing Form*, and has worked on the backstretch and been a horse owner. Morrison has won the Sovereign Award twice for outstanding writing.

Claire Novak is a Lexington, Kentucky-based journalist whose work appears in a variety of print and online publications, including NBCsports.com, *The Blood-Horse* magazine, *The Horse Player*, *Louisville*, and *Keeneland* magazine. A member of the National Turf Writers' Association, she has covered racing for the Associated Press and various newspapers.

Sherry Pinson is director of communications for Turfway Park racetrack in northern Kentucky. As a freelance writer and editor, Pinson has served regional, national, and international corporate clients in a variety of industries. She is the author of two books, one on humanitarian and mission work in Appalachia and Baja California and a second on drug and alcohol rehabilitation ministries in Ukraine.

Josh Pons is a fifth-generation Maryland horseman and a two-time Eclipse award-winning author. His family farm, Country Life, was the farm where the famous racehorse Cigar was foaled and is Maryland's oldest Thoroughbred nursery. Pons is the author of *Merryland: Two Years in the Life of a Racing Stable* and *Country Life Diary*.

Virginia Preston is a lifelong horsewoman who lives on a Jessamine County, Kentucky, farm with her husband, two sons, and various creatures great and small. A former competitor in jumpers and eventing, she now is content with foxhunting and trail riding.

Alicia Wincze is the turf writer for the Lexington (Kentucky) *Herald-Leader* and a former staff writer for *Thoroughbred Times* magazine. She began riding at the age of eight in her native Connecticut and was a four-year member of the Pace University Equestrian Team in Pleasantville, New York.